Words that Sing

GAIL RAMSHAW

LITURGY TRAINING PUBLICATIONS

Printed in the United States of America.

Editor: Elizabeth Hoffman
Editorial assistance: Theresa Pincich, Lorraine Schmidt
Design: Mary Bowers
Typesetting: Mark Hollopeter

The illustrations on the cover and throughout the book are from an unpublished manuscript of hymns written by Johannes Kelpius in 1706. Kelpius wrote the hymns for his community, The Brotherhood of the Woman in the Wilderness, also known as The Wissahickon Hermits because they resided in the Wissahickon Valley in southeastern Pennsylvania.

Words That Sing is typeset in Palatino and Univers. Initial capitals are reproduced from *Decorative Alphabets Throughout the Ages* by Pat Russell (© Studio Editions, 1988).

ISBN 0-929650-42-5

on the Visitation,
to two other singers, Miriam and Monica,
that these hymns may be theirs

CONTENTS

THE YEAR: ORDINARY TIME

What Is a Hymn?

The actions of the Christian liturgy are undergirded and surmounted with words. Words narrate the gospel, which the meal enacts. Words give explicit Christian interpretation to otherwise commonplace rituals like the bath and the handshake. The liturgy is not merely words: We cannot experience a liturgy by reading its text, and parishes speaking identical words conduct quite dissimilar events. Yet the words remain essential.

In the liturgy, a majority of the words are sung. Like ritual speech in many of the world's religions, Christian liturgical language reaches out for melody and rhythm. The "Holy Holy Holy" lies on the floor of the sanctuary if spoken, but can rise to the heights it describes if sung. Listen to the whooping of a Baptist preacher, whose voice raises in pitch and whose speech quickens until finally the sermon breaks out in exuberant melody, speech become chant become song. Our service music includes even sung dialogue, the notes adding a dimension to the historic responses.

Much of the sung liturgy is "the ordinary," those responses and songs that recur ordinarily at the weekly eucharist. Indeed, some Roman Catholic liturgical scholars teach that "the ordinary" and the appointed biblical antiphons and refrains are all that should be sung, that the metrical songs we call hymns have no place at all in the eucharist. Surely the biblicism of this position, like that of the early Calvinists, calls us to the highest excellence in liturgical texts, and for this reminder of our roots we are grateful. But it is also said that the eucharistic rite is a single flowing form which hymns interrupt; that the eucharist is action, and a hymn is not action; that hymns are prone either to didacticism or to excessive poetry; and that churches who prize hymnody neglect the psalter.

Surely, when hymns are poorly written, poorly composed, poorly chosen, and poorly sung, such a reaction is understandable; and of course hymns ought not displace psalms. But finally this strict position, heard mostly from clergy, does not appreciate the profound role that hymns, if written, composed, chosen and sung well, play in the people's worship. The liturgy is not ministerial action to which the people attend; and to suggest that the eucharistic order of, say, the 6th century, is the epitome of liturgical flow is to ignore those traditions in Orthodoxy, historic Lutheranism, several centuries of Anglicanism, and recent Methodism and Presbyterianism, in which the people's eucharistic practice has been deeply enriched by superb hymnody.

Hymns are part of the liturgy's "propers." Proper to the specific liturgy and the liturgical season, hymns grant the assembly a vigorous communal participation in the uniqueness of each eucharistic celebration. Many of the variables in the liturgy—the bids in the Kyrie, the presider's prayers, the proper preface, the vestments' color— the people only hear or see. But in the several hymns the voices of the people shape the proper Sunday. These hymns may be scheduled at various places in the liturgy: to focus the assembly at the outset of the liturgy, to accompany processions, to respond to the gospel in a "hymn of the day," to provide meditative texts during the communion, or to give the assembly a rousing leave-taking. In daily prayer there may be a hymn proper to the time of day and one proper to the season or reading. Some assemblies find one substantial hymn enough, while for others, without at least four hymns of four stanzas each, one hardly feels as if one has been to church.

Some scholars find it helpful to distinguish among various types of communal song. Perhaps inspired by the comment in Ephesians about "psalms and hymns and spiritual songs," this categorizing usually defines hymns as metrical and imaginative congregational song. According to this strict definition, hymns are not ballads, folk songs, spirituals or mantras, nor are they canticles or versified psalms. With such categories in place, one can argue when the precise genre "hymn" is appropriate and when not.

Although judgment concerning hymns is essential, it is finally not according to such categories that appropriateness lies. While some centuries of the church produced sequence hymns, others wrote folk songs. While some pieties sang spirituals, others chanted mantras. While some denominations were restricted to biblical versification, others welcomed imaginative lyrics. In this ecumenical age we can benefit from this wide variety of genres. Whether we choose a fourth-century office hymn, a sixteenth-century chorale or an African American spiritual, our intent is the same: to select the most appropriate propers for the assembly. In this book the word "hymn" functions as a broad term to refer to the assembly's song adorning the ordinary of the liturgy.

The church's collection of hymns is an ecumenical treasure. In the hymn-singing traditions, hymns become central to the people's piety. Hymns are the primary way that the liturgical year and theological imagery are appropriated by the laity. Thus a wealth of denominationally distinct hymnody exists; and while recent hymnals have been marked by ecumenical inclusivity, each denomination rightly publishes its own preferences in spirituality. In identifying our distinct charisms, we all search for the best hymns in our tradition. Yet none of us stands in royal isolation any longer, and while we honor our own distinctive historic patterns, the age is past when we hide within our tradition, refusing to learn from each other. In singing one another's hymns we are opened up to one another's spirituality. Happily the notion that Roman Catholics after Vatican II needed to compose all their own new hymnody has given way to an ecumenical donning of the jewels that make up the Christian hymn treasury.

Such opening up occurs not only across denominational lines, as when Roman Catholics sing a Wesley hymn or Episcopalians revive a Shaker song. Hymns also open up our narrow present to the hundreds of years of piety that went before us. It is not easy to decide which past spirituality to put our voices around. A hymn must not force on the assembly a piety so alien that the people who are thinking about the words quit singing in disgust. Some hymns are marked by images now offensive or language irretrievably sexist. We no longer sing the old mission hymn about "pagan priests" or that monument to nineteenth-century American piety, "If Men Go to Hell, Who Cares." These hymns must join our academic preaching gowns and golden monstrances in a museum. Although hymns give us the occasion to sing images and sentiments we would not speak, we will not sing what we consider absolute untruths.

Singing the hymns of the past involves mind-splitting issues. How much ought we adapt an archaic image to our time? On the other hand, when is it enriching to recall a previous worldview? The question is easy; the answering, arduous. Sometimes the past deepens our spirituality with the faith of our forebears, but sometimes the past is already putrid and needs to be buried immediately. Of our hundreds of hymns, some can retain their archaisms, and some must be adapted by contemporary equivalents. Hymns written in languages other than English require periodic retranslation: In this way the obsolete "generic masculine" can yield to the inclusive community, and by changing the third person to second person address, our language for God can move toward wholeness.

The hymns of the past can free us from the prison of ourselves. If all we had were the words of our decade and the tunes of our generation, our praise would be impoverished, especially during an age such as ours when our focus is obsessively on the self. The pieties of the past enrich our song with words and images we may have overlooked, with fervor we may have forgotten, with lament we imagine we have outgrown. A dynamic way to be illumined by the brilliance of the saints is to sing their songs, and many's the time a profound hymn text based on the gospel reading has refocused a liturgy after a less-than-profound homily.

The great hymns of the past, those ten masterpieces per century, are balanced by new compositions. Some recent compositions expand our sense of what a hymn is, as we add mantras, African melodies or bilingual songs to our repertoire. Some new texts speak to a new liturgical awareness, such as the baptismal content of Lent for which there is very little classic hymnody. Other new hymns fill the gaps in our forebears' imagination. Lest our oppressive overabundance of masculine hierarchical imagery for God bludgeon feminists out of the church, we need to sing praise to God as Sophia and Tree of Life. The church must encourage the best hymnwriters alive, holding them responsible for today's expression of lively Christian orthodoxy.

Several unhelpful tendencies, however, are recurring in the stacks of newly composed hymnody. Some hymns are marked by mediocre scriptural knowledge or erroneous theology. Some are smitten by immature emotion. Some are obsessive "cause songs" which mean to induce in the assembly the estimable attitudes of the hymnwriter. The assembly rightly feels exhausted after participating in such browbeating. Some hymn texts, modeled after twentieth-century poetry, are far too dense to be accessible for the singing congregation. One innovation that deserves absolute censure is the "I am God" hymnody, in which the assembly, pretending to be God, sings some supposed divine words. Those hymns which snuggle up to God as my best buddy might perhaps first kneel before the mystery of the divine. Easy anthropomorphisms lean toward idolatry by depicting God in our own image.

Hymns sung by the assembly may be rendered in such an anemic manner as to weaken the whole event, or they may be so robust that they enliven the liturgy and support the rest of the propers. But the faithful are no fools; they will not sing heartily sappy songs and inconsequential ditties. Hymns will not succeed as confectioners' sugar dusted on top of the waffles. Hymns will succeed if with profound texts, enduring melody and memorable rhythm they enable the assembly's hearty participation in the liturgy. We must locate those hymns, ancient and modern, that are worthy of their high task. Jonathan Edwards wrote, "Praise is the Act of Intelligent Creatures, and not the act of mere machines or things without life; nor is it properly Praise, though it be done by Intelligent Creatures, except it be done intelligently." Through which hymns can we sing intelligent praise?

One quality that renders great hymns intelligent as communal expression is their tendency to be metaphoric rather than subjective. That is, hymns contain metaphors, objective images that give space for the community to move around in. A text that describes the Christian life as the Exodus, baptismal water as a pool in the desert or the cross as a blossoming tree provides a place for the 7-year-old, the 17-year-old and the 70-year-old. There is room in a metaphor for the contented as well as for the dispirited, for the healthy as well as for the dying. Less successful are hymns that detail a subjective emotion, presupposing sorrow or happiness or contrition. Precise descriptions of emotional states limit a text's usefulness in the diverse assembly, which is far from emotionally unified on any specific Sunday.

Hymns for intelligent praise choose corporate rather than personal expression. Although we live in an extremely individualistic culture, for the liturgy we need to identify those texts that construe the assembly as *we*, not merely a momentary collection of *I*'s. My individual condition and my private emotion are tempered by the Christian assembly. My contentment must face another's misery, my favorite metaphors must yield to communally available imagery. The Christian assembly is shaped by the Spirit of the resurrected life, not by the mood of the parish musician or the preferences of the presider. This "we" need not be literal, but it is a quality of the text. The psalms, our great teachers, often have an "I" that is the body, the whole assembly.

Hymns for intelligent praise must be able to be sung by regular folk. We are told that the vast majority of American Christians sing communally only at corporate worship. Since we do not sing together, not even our ungainly national anthem, we cannot extrapolate from the secular world the best form, melody and rhythm for hymnody. During the decade of the post–Vatican II reforms, popular music was in the so-called "folk idiom," characterized by melodic tunes and participatory refrains with guitar-led accompaniment. But such "folk music" is no longer the dominant popular music in the United States. Even while it lasted, the folk style was perhaps too introspective and gentle to sustain much hearty congregational song. We sing during a time of no consensus concerning musical style for the liturgy.

Liturgical song tends to acquire instrumental accompaniment. In the second century, Clement of Alexandria wrote, "If you want to sing and praise God to the music of the cithara or the lyre, it is not blameworthy." In subsequent centuries, however, instrumental music was banned from eucharistic worship because the instruments were associated with pagan religious rites and secular theater. As the centuries progressed, the hierarchy had to issue repeated injunctions against instrumental music, for strings kept making their way back into the liturgy. By the thirteenth century, organs were becoming common in parts of Europe, the size of church buildings necessitating not soft strings but resounding pipes. Pipe organs were important in establishing robust singing in the Reformation churches. To complete the circle, folk music brought strings back again to accompany the assembly's song. There is currently no consensus concerning which strings and pipes are ideal for accompanying twentieth-century assemblies.

Guided by these principles and goaded by these questions, this book considers 40 such intelligent hymns. These hymns were chosen, not because they are my favorites, but because through them we experience the astounding diversity of Christian congregational song. Since we choose hymns as each Sunday's propers, this book is organized around the liturgical year. Our hymns represent dozens of spiritual traditions. This book attends to an office hymn from the third century, antiphons from the ninth, sequence hymns and processional hymns from the Middle Ages, a carol from the fourteenth, chorales from the sixteenth, a marching song from the nineteenth. Lest we get bored, add an eighteenth-century ballad adapted from a Jewish catechism, a Calvinist versified psalm, an African American spiritual and a chant from a Shaker dance.

Ideally, the classic and the new with their variety of strings and pipes all find their place in the liturgy. Hymns enrich our doctrinal emphasis with that of another tradition, our spirituality with that of a previous age, my emotion with that of my neighbors, our musical taste with that of another culture. Hymns must be in some way our words, our tunes, even my words and tunes; yet in the liturgy our words and tunes are bigger and deeper and older than they are outside the liturgy, and hymnody helps achieve that goal.

While some Christians lived and died without a strong hymn tradition, we need not emulate their poverty. Hymns, while givers of life, will not stay alive on their own. It is our parish musicians and planning committees who must schedule their use, our presiders who must respect these profound contributions to the people's piety, our assemblies who must sing their throats hoarse. In our singing, we keep the saints' words among us.

A story of one such saint, before we begin studying intelligent hymns: Anna Hoppe was a Lutheran stenographer who lived in Milwaukee during the early years of this century. During her lunch hours she used the office typewriter to compose hymns. In 1928, she published *Songs for the Church Year*, which included one hymn based on each gospel and another on each epistle for the old one-year lectionary. Her aspiration was to compose 1,000 hymns; she completed about 500. Her one surviving hymn, based on Mark 7:31–37, praises the God who in Jesus healed the man's speech impediment and frees our "speechless tongue." I want us today to remember her: a Lutheran laywoman, hoping that with lively scriptural hymnody the assembly's tongue would find the words to sing out the year of grace.

THE DAY

. . . as forward we travel from light into light . . .

"Let all things now living,"
Katherine Davis

O Radiant Light (Phos hilaron)

O radiant Light, O Sun divine
　　of God the Father's deathless face,
O image of the Light sublime
that fills the heavenly dwelling place,

O Son of God, the source of life,
praise is your due by night and day.
Our happy lips must raise the strain
of your esteemed and splendid name.

Lord Jesus Christ, as daylight fades,
as shine the lights of eventide,
we praise the Father with the Son,
the Spirit blest, and with them one.

anon., tr. William G. Storey

O Splendor of God's Glory Bright

O splendor of God's glory bright,
from light eternal bringing light;
thou light of life, light's living spring,
true day, all days illumining:

Come, Holy Sun of heavenly love,
shower down thy radiance from above,
and to our inward hearts convey
the Holy Spirit's cloudless ray.

O joyful be the passing day
with thoughts as clear as morning's ray,
with faith like noontide shining bright,
our souls unshadowed by the night.

O Lord, with each returning morn
thine image to our hearts is born;
O may we ever clearly see
our Savior and our God in thee!

Ambrose, tr. composite

Awake, My Soul

Awake, my soul, and with the sun
thy daily stage of duty run;
shake off dull sloth, and joyful rise
to pay thy morning sacrifice.

All praise to thee, who safe hast kept
and hast refreshed me while I slept.
Grant, Lord, when I from death shall wake,
I may of endless light partake.

Lord, I my vows to thee renew.
Disperse my sins as morning dew;
guard my first springs of thought and will,
and with thyself my spirit fill.

Direct, control, suggest, this day,
all I design or do or say,
that all my powers, with all their might,
in thy sole glory may unite.

Praise God, from whom all blessings flow;
praise God, all creatures here below;
praise God above, ye heavenly host;
praise Father, Son, and Holy Ghost.

Thomas Ken

All Praise to Thee

All praise to thee, my God, this night,
for all the blessings of the light!
Keep me, O keep me, King of kings,
beneath thine own almighty wings.

Forgive me, Lord, for thy dear Son,
the ill that I this day have done,
that with the world, myself, and thee,
I, ere I sleep, at peace may be.

Teach me to live, that I may dread
the grave as little as my bed.
Teach me to die, that so I may
rise glorious at the judgment day.

O may my soul on thee repose,
and with sweet sleep mine eyelids close,
sleep that may me more vigorous make
to serve my God when I awake.

Praise God, from whom all blessings flow;
praise God, all creatures here below;
praise God above, ye heavenly host;
praise Father, Son, and Holy Ghost.

Thomas Ken

For millenia, religions have instructed the faithful to frame their day with prayer. To awake is to be born again to life, and thus religious folk praise the Creator for another new day and beg for health and safety. To fall asleep in peace is to trust the darkness; so religious folk rest assured in the comfort granted by their deity. Christians learned from Jews this pattern of praise and petition at the beginning and ending of the day, and a body of hymns has arisen to assist this prayer.

What marks specifically Christian prayer at dawn and dusk is Christ. We plead with the almighty and merciful God to give us safety through the turns of life. But rather than the dangers of day and night being central, Christ is central. Nature's cycle becomes not only an opportunity for enrichment or the threat of disaster but a symbol of Christ. The morning reminds us of God's creation of the world and its re-creation in Christ; the lamp in the night is an emblem of Christ and Easter's resurrection. Christians incorporate their prayer for safety and health into their praise for the deeper life of grace.

We see this pattern in the Christian practice of singing the Benedictus in the morning and the Magnificat at night. Zechariah's Benedictus is a rousing song, perhaps originating in the Maccabean period, a warrior's praise of a victorious God who will this very day fight with us against our enemies. Yet the canticle's conclusion admits that the day's light comes not with our victory, or even with the sun, but in the coming of the compassionate one, who will lead our march into the way of peace. The Lucan narrative of John the Baptist's birth says that out of Zechariah's silence comes the warrior's cheer, a victory cry in anticipation of God's arrival.

The same pattern is present in the evening. We discover at nightfall that we have not vanquished all our foes; we are defenseless again before the powers of night. Thus the Christian day concludes with Mary's Magnificat, the song of the serving woman. She goes gently into the good night, trusting that along with all the terrified of the world she will not only survive, but in God's mercy she will conquer. Again, it is not safety through the darkness that she lauds but the surprising mercy of God in Christ.

Among the most ancient hymns extant from the early Christian community are songs that copy the Benedictus and the Magnificat in framing the day. The oldest of them is the "Phos hilaron." Already called "ancient" in the year 370, this Greek hymn exemplifies Christian marking of the evening. The hymn describes the community's ritual of evening lamp lighting—surely a powerful sign of divine presence in the eras before electricity. Reminiscent of the paschal candle at the Easter Vigil, the vesper lamp is praised as a sign of Christ, who is a gladsome light and the divine sunlight within the faithful community.

The hymn is sheer praise. The faithful have need of nothing, for their life even during the night hours is safe in the Trinity. The imagery is based on the Trinity: as the Son comes from the Father, so light comes from God for all the faithful people. Christ is both the Sun divine and the Son of God. In the Germanic languages, English included, the imagery is strengthened by the pun of son-sun. English-speaking Christians have no need of sun, having already the Son.

Nearly all recent hymnals publish at least one setting of the "Phos hilaron." For the melody, some settings adapt a plainsong chant, others use a fifteenth-century hymn tune called Nunc Dimittis. Some versions— "O gladsome light of the Father immortal," "O radiant light," "Joyous light of glory"—translate the hymn as accurately as possible, thus utilizing the Father-Son, sunlight imagery. Other versions—"O gladsome light, O grace," "O laughing light"—stress the creation of light, avoiding the Father language. In either case, the hymn remains strongly Christocentric, a song with which to close the day in Christ.

In the third and fourth centuries, much of Christendom was bilingual, the educated classes writing in Greek and the common people speaking Latin. Thus when Ambrose composed hymns for the people to sing, he wrote in Latin. Ambrose was the enormously popular bishop of Milan who while Roman consul—the story is astounding—was chosen bishop even before his baptism and who, short and droopy-eyed though he was, went on to stand up to empress and emperor both. How could Ambrose solidify public support against the empress's Arian belief that Christ was a demigod, a half-human, half-divine mediator between the two realms? Ambrose wrote brilliant hymns, with clear Latin and spirited rhythm, and the people sang and sang of Christ, fully human and fully divine.

Ambrose's morning hymn, "O splendor of God's glory bright," written for the people to sing at the morning office, is reminiscent of the "Phos hilaron." The sun is rising, and we laud this reminder of Christ the light. The divine radiance we see showering down is the ray of the Holy Spirit. Our true light is our life in the Trinity. Ambrose was a master of metaphor: Read his sermons and his catechetical lectures and be blown away by his metaphors for the Christian life. But like the brocade vestments covering up his bones at his glass tomb in Milan, our English verse obscures his supreme clarity, and translations can sound archaic or convoluted. Some hymnals assign Ambrose's hymn to a plainsong chant, but others, like the current Methodist and Presbyterian hymnals, replace the plainsong with easy and familiar long meter tunes, thus hoping to revive the simple popularity of Ambrose's hymns.

Exit Bishop Ambrose and his Empress Justinia, and 1,300 years later, enter Bishop Thomas Ken and King Charles II. It is the close of the seventeeth century in England, when the Tower of London still imprisoned pious Catholics one decade, pious Protestants the next, Bishop Ken among them. Thomas Ken was like Ambrose in a number of ways: He publicly condemned royalty, and he pioneered in writing hymns in his vernacular. Anglicans did not sing congregational hymns in public worship during Ken's lifetime, but the boys at boarding school did at their morning and evening devotions, and for these students Ken wrote two of the most renowned hymns for morning and evening prayer in English, "Awake, my soul, and with the sun" and "All praise to Thee, my God, this night."

The ancient office hymns from the Greek and Latin take the occasion of night and day to offer praise to Christ. By contrast, these later hymns by Ken are compact intercessory prayers. "Awake, my soul," always sung to the lively tune entitled Morning Hymn, includes a call to praise, thanksgiving for safety and petition for guidance through the day. The evening hymn, beloved for its setting as a round to the Tallis Canon, includes a prayer for safety, a plea for forgiveness and a petition for rest in God. In Ken's verse we see that Christians have added to their Christological praise the more primitive religious stance, pleading to the divine for comfort and blessing at the turns of night and day.

Both Thomas Ken and Ambrose criticized the throne and wrote hymns in the vernacular, but there is yet another similarity between the two bishops. Ken agreed with Ambrose that it is in the Trinity that we rest securely; in Trinitarian praise is our peace. So he concluded both his morning and his evening hymns with a stanza that has become the most famous doxology in English: "Praise God, from whom all blessings flow." It is relatively easy for us to edit out the masculine pronouns:

> Praise God, from whom all blessings flow;
> praise God, all creatures here below;
> praise God above, ye heavenly host:
> praise Father, Son, and Holy Ghost.

Let us keep this doxology alive and well among us. I like to think of Ambrose learning English by joining us in Thomas Ken's praise.

THE WEEK

. . . We are God's house of living stones . . .

"Built on a rock,"
Nicolai Grundtvig

All Creatures of Our God and King

All creatures of our God and King,
lift up your voice and with us sing,
    O praise ye! Alleluia!
O brother sun with golden beam,
O sister moon with silver gleam!
    O praise ye! O praise ye! Alleluia! Alleluia! Alleluia!

O brother wind, air, clouds, and rain,
by which all creatures ye sustain,
    O praise ye! Alleluia!
Thou rising morn, in praise rejoice,
ye lights of evening, find a voice!
    O praise ye! O praise ye! Alleluia! Alleluia! Alleluia!

O sister water, flowing clear,
make music for thy Lord to hear,
    Alleluia! Alleluia!
O brother fire who lights the night,
providing warmth, enhancing sight!
    O praise ye! O praise ye! Alleluia! Alleluia! Alleluia!

Dear mother earth, who day by day
unfoldest blessings on our way,
  Alleluia! Alleluia!
The flowers and fruits that in thee grow,
let them God's glory also show!
  O praise ye! O praise ye! Alleluia! Alleluia! Alleluia!

All ye who are of tender heart,
forgiving others, take your part,
  O praise ye! Alleluia!
Ye who long pain and sorrow bear,
praise God and on God cast your care!
  O praise ye! O praise ye! Alleluia! Alleluia! Alleluia!

And thou, our sister, gentle death,
waiting to hush our latest breath,
  Alleluia! Alleluia!
Thou leadest home the child of God,
and Christ our Lord the way has trod,
  O praise ye! O praise ye! Alleluia! Alleluia! Alleluia!

Let all things their Creator bless,
and worship God in humbleness,
    O praise ye! Alleluia!
Praise, praise the Father, praise the Son,
and praise the Spirit, Three in One!
    O praise ye! O praise ye! Alleluia! Alleluia! Alleluia!

Francis of Assisi, tr. William Draper, alt.

Hope of the World

Hope of the world, thou Christ of great compassion:
speak to our fearful hearts by conflict rent.
Save us, thy people, from consuming passion,
who by our own false hopes and aims are spent.

Hope of the world, God's gift from highest heaven,
bringing to hungry souls the bread of life:
still let thy Spirit unto us be given
to heal earth's wounds and end our bitter strife.

Hope of the world, afoot on dusty highways,
showing to wand'ring souls the path of light:
walk thou beside us lest the tempting byways
lure us away from thee to endless night.

Hope of the world, who by thy cross didst save us
from death and dark despair, from sin and guilt:
we render back the love thy mercy gave us;
take thou our lives and use them as thou wilt.

Hope of the world, O Christ, o'er death victorious,
why by this sign didst conquer grief and pain:
we would be faithful to thy Gospel glorious;
thou art our Lord! Thou dost forever reign!

Georgia Harkness

On Sunday, Justin wrote in 150 CE, God created light and Christ rose from the dead. Because of this, Christians assemble on Sunday to praise God's light and Christ's resurrection. Christians are accustomed to singing Sunday praise: Whether in the classic "Glory to God" or in one of hundreds of praise hymns, the choirs or the people orient weekly worship with praise. We inherit this pattern from the Jews before us. The solemn assembly described in Nehemiah 9 is one example of God's people uniting in praise of a creating, saving deity.

Close to praise is lament. As in the great prayer in Nehemiah 9, when the paragraphs of praise are completed, the petitions commence. "Now, therefore, our God": Since you have heard our praise, now heed our plea. We humans lament our lot before the Divine. We are hungry, we are sick, we will die, there is war, much is evil. Surely a god with the power to create and the mercy to save will again act beneficently toward a needy people. So we lament.

But just as praise opens the door for lament, lament always turns back to praise. Even the psalm of ultimate despair, "My God, my God, why have you forsaken me," concludes with praise. The praise and lament are two pitches in the same cry, two melodic lines in the same song. The classic Roman collects follow the same pattern: O God, who has shown great mercy in the past, show now yet more mercy to us in our distress. Praise and lament, lament and praise.

We thank Francis of Assisi for one of our magnificent hymns of praise. While many Christian hymns praise God for salvation, Francis's famous Canticle of Brother Sun, one of the very few pieces of writing uncontestably his own, praises God for the whole of creation. The version best known among us was translated early in this century by William Draper. A recent adaptation of this version not only eliminates the repeated masculine references to God but also renders the words more closely to the spirit of Francis.

Francis composed the hymn in his Umbrian Italian dialect, and the ambiguous prepositions in his poem, *cum* and *per*, can be translated in different ways. God can be praised for all of creation, or through the created order, or by the creatures. Draper's translation, by calling on the sun and moon to offer their praise, makes the hymn more romantic than Francis's was. Francis was more than our birdbaths suggest, a dreamer communing with the animals. Rather, by focusing on the faith of the individual rather than on the life of the hierarchical church, he was a catalyst for the beginning of a popular lay spirituality. He cultivated an incarnational piety fruitful for the common believers. In Francis's text, God is praised over and over for all of the world in which every believer lives and dies. By the way, "King" does not occur in Francis's text but obviously was incorporated into the line to rhyme with "sing." We need a translation free from nineteenth-century thought patterns, one more authentically Francis's.

As our century turns away from a careless exploitation of nature toward its care and veneration, Francis's hymn is newly appropriate in our praises. Although the archetypal pattern of giving gender designations to the things of nature is now a debatable issue, we can at least occasionally recall the ancient imagery of brother sun and sister moon, brother wind, sister water and mother earth. Francis's point is not to classify human beings through a supposed likeness to nature but to give words to a creation spirituality, one that is critical for our time.

But Francis's canticle is not merely the song of a happy camper. Francis wrote the poem not while youthfully running through the flowery fields but in 1225, a year before his death, in midwinter, while nearly blind and enduring excruciating pain in head and belly. He was in a state of lament, and yet he praised. Stanza six is central for the intensity of the hymn: Even "our sister, gentle death, waiting to hush our latest breath," is praising God.

As flourishing life is a sign of God's majesty, so is imminent death another faithful creature of God.

We are used to praising. The Francises among us can praise even in a state of lament. But we are poor at lament. Perhaps Christianity turned too soon and too completely to prayers for forgiveness of sin, so overwhelming was its piety with sorrow for sin that there was no energy left for other lament. Thus while our traditions offer dozens, hundreds, of hymns about personal or corporate sin, there are practically no hymns of genuine lament, litanies that beg God on behalf of a world marked by pain, poverty, war and death, texts that present before God the countless sorrows of the world.

One rare hymn does. If dying Francis, who although having much to lament, wrote exuberant praise, we encounter the opposite in "Hope of the world." Georgia Harkness was a dynamic twentieth-century American Methodist laywoman. She worked tirelessly for equality for women, for social concerns, for a renewal of spirituality, for a world of peace. She was the first woman in this country to hold a full professorship at a theological seminary. In 1954, inspired by the joyous occasion of the Second General Assembly of the World Council of Churches, she wrote a hymn, but she had the wisdom and breadth to lament.

How is our century characterized in this hymn? People are fearful, wounded, warring wanderers, consumed by passion, spent by false hopes, marked by grief, pain and despair. The text calls us to a deeper level of truth. We are shown the pain below the smiles, the agonies present among us, even when as individuals we are the first to achieve yet another goal. The hymn does not pray for instant deliverance; all will not be perfect. But we beg: Speak to our hearts; bring food to the hungry; walk with the wandering; save us from despair. Christ is hope, compassion, bread, light and guide for our struggling life. God reigns; the hymn does not imagine that we will.

When we have Georgia Harkness's lament in the marrow of our bones, those bones can dance more joyously with Francis's praise. Perhaps like Francis we are lying in pain, awaiting death—let us praise. Perhaps like Georgia we are flying around the country serving on another committee—let us lament. These two lay Christians can help the assembly to praise and lament, lament and praise. For the assembly is always deeper than the words of a man dying or a woman living, more profound than one man praising and one woman lamenting. We are both, every Sunday, praise and lament, lament and praise.

The God of Abraham Praise

The God of Abraham praise,
who reigns enthroned above;
ancient of everlasting days,
and God of love.
Jehovah, great I Am!
by earth and heaven confessed;
I bow and bless the sacred name,
forever blest.

The God of Abraham praise,
at whose supreme command
from earth I rise and seek the joys
at his right hand.
I all on earth forsake—
its wisdom, fame, and power—
and him my only portion make,
my shield and tower.

The God of Abraham praise,
whose all sufficient grace
shall guide me all my pilgrim days
in all my ways.

He deigns to call me friend;
he calls himself my God!
And he shall save me to the end
through Jesus' blood.

He by himself has sworn;
I on his oath depend.
I shall, on eagle wings upborne,
to heaven ascend.
I shall behold his face;
I shall his power adore,
and sing the wonders of his grace
forevermore.

Though nature's strength decay,
and earth and hell withstand,
to Canaan's bounds I urge my way
at his command.
The watery deep I pass,
with Jesus in my view,
and through the howling wilderness
my way pursue.

The goodly land I see,
with peace and plenty blest;
a land of sacred liberty,
and endless rest.
There milk and honey flow,
and oil and wine abound,
and trees of life forever grow
with mercy crowned.

There dwells the Lord our king,
the Lord our righteousness,
triumphant over the world and sin,
the prince of peace.
On Zion's sacred height,
his kingdom he maintains,
and glorious with his saints in light
forever reigns.

Before the great Three-One
they all exulting stand
and tell the wonders he has done
through all their land.

The listening spheres attend
and swell the growing fame
and sing the songs which never end,
the wondrous name.

The God who reigns on high
the great archangels sing,
and "Holy, holy, holy!" cry,
"Almighty King!
Who was, and is, the same,
and evermore shall be:
Jehovah, Father, great I Am!
we worship thee!"

Before the Savior's face
the ransomed nations bow,
o'erwhelmed at his almighty grace
forever new.
He shows his wounds of love;
they kindle to a flame!
and sound through all the worlds above
the Paschal Lamb.

The whole triumphant host
give thanks to God on high.
"Hail, Father, Son, and Holy Ghost!"
they ever cry.
Hail, Abraham's God and mine!
I join the heavenly lays:
all might and majesty are thine
and endless praise!

adp. Thomas Olivers, alt.

From Heaven Above

From heaven above to earth I come
 to bring good news to everyone!
Glad tidings of great joy I bring
to all the world, and gladly sing:

To you this night is born a child
of Mary, chosen virgin mild;
this newborn child of lowly birth
shall be the joy of all the earth.

This is the Christ, God's Son most high,
who hears your sad and bitter cry;
he will himself your Savior be
and from all sin will set you free.

The blessing which the Father planned
the Son holds in his infant hand,
that in his kingdom, bright and fair,
you may with us his glory share.

These are the signs which you will see
to let you know that it is he:
in manger-bed, in swaddling clothes
the child who all the earth upholds.

How glad we'll be to find it so!
Then with the shepherds let us go
to see what God for us has done
in sending us his own dear Son.

Look, look, dear friends, look over there!
What lies within that manger bare?
Who is that lovely little one?
The baby Jesus, God's dear Son.

Welcome to earth, O noble Guest,
through whom this sinful world is blest!
You turned not from our needs away!
How can our thanks such love repay?

O Lord, you have created all!
How did you come to be so small,
to sweetly sleep in manger-bed
where lowing cattle lately fed?

Where earth a thousand times as fair
and set with gold and jewels rare,
still such a cradle would not do
to rock a prince so great as you.

For velvets soft and silken stuff
you have but hay and straw so rough
on which as king so rich and great
to be enthroned in humble state.

O dearest Jesus, holy child,
prepare a bed, soft, undefiled,
a holy shrine, within my heart,
that you and I need never part.

My heart for very joy now leaps;
my voice no longer silence keeps;
I too must join the angel-throng
to sing with joy his cradle-song:

"Glory to God in highest heaven,
who unto us his Son has given."
With angels sing in pious mirth:
a glad new year to all the earth!

Martin Luther, tr. composite

The first of the two pivotal events in the weekly Christian assembly is the reading of the word. In that word are the sounds of God's merciful speech, narratives of the faithful—and unfaithful—people, and accounts of apostolic belief. The assembly hears the words of the gospels, the Hebrew scriptures and the epistles, and calls out, "Thanks be to God!" For to hear these words is to have our communal identity affirmed and our individual place in that community strengthened. We are the people who hear these stories. We are the people whose backbone is formed by these segments and links.

When I was a child our car had no CD player, our kitchen had no radio, there were no Walkmans: Thus while we drove to state parks or washed dishes or walked home from school with mother, we sang together, long ballads, 10-stanza hymns in harmony and add-on nonsense songs. The singing was a communal adventure, as hearing recorded music seldom is. In stanza after stanza of profound or silly song, the family was held together by the words, the tune, the very experience of singing. I can remember the decades: "The Ballad of Davy Crockett," all 19 stanzas of "The Ballad of Holy History," "Puff the Magic Dragon" and, throughout, the duel between Abdul Abul-Bul Amir and Ivan Skavinsky Skavar.

The church has its ballads, songs with many stanzas from distant centuries that narrate the stories we hear in the readings. Bede in the eighth century wrote our 8-stanza "A Hymn of Glory" about the ascension; from the thirteenth century comes the Stabat Mater, with its 15-stanza narration of Mary at the cross; from the fifteenth century Jean Tisserand brings us the 9-stanza "O sons and daughters" about Christ's appearance to Thomas; and from Thomas à Kempis we have 7 stanzas of "O Love, how deep," a creedal narration of the life of Christ. Stanza after stanza spins out the tales, allowing the assembly to make the sacred stories its own.

One such ballad is "The God of Abraham praise." Many of our hymnals contain it, but only one includes 11 of the 12 stanzas. This ballad, a prototype of the Christian reading of Hebrew scripture, has a fascinating history. The hymn began in the twelfth century, when the Jewish scholar Moses Maimonides compiled the 13 articles of Jewish faith. Two centuries later, the liturgical poet Daniel ben Judah versified the creed into a 13-stanza Hebrew doxology called Yigdal. Four centuries after that, Thomas Olivers, an English shoemaker turned evangelist through the influence of John and Charles Wesley, heard Yigdal sung by a famed cantor in a London synagogue. He adapted the Hebrew poem for Christian use in the hymn he titled "The God of Abraham praise." The Hebrew scriptures become Jewish creed become synagogue praise become Christian praise: The hymn is worthy of our continued attention.

As is often the case, antiquity surprises us with its contemporaneity. The current century can sometimes find amenable practices or metaphors in centuries long past. This old Christian hymn retains the Jewish practice of praising God's sacred name by the very modern practice of recalling many divine metaphors. The God of love is imaged as monarch, ancient of days, I AM, our portion, shield, tower, guide, friend, righteousness. In stanza four we approach the face of God "on eagle wings upborne"; in stanza seven the God who triumphs over the world and sin is the prince of peace; in stanza eight we praise the "Three-One"; in stanza ten, the paschal lamb. The remaining stanzas tell the narrative of God's pilgrim people, traveling through the wilderness, arriving in the promised land and dwelling in the kingdom. Whenever would we sing a ballad with 11 stanzas? Anytime, everytime: Especially those weeks when the readings recall our heritage in the faith of Abraham, this saga would be appropriate. We sing these Jewish-Christian words to a Jewish chant, for the tune, named Yigdal, is adapted from the synagogue chant which the London cantor transcribed for Thomas Olivers.

Another such biblical ballad—this one has 14 stanzas—is Martin Luther's Christmas hymn "From heaven above." Luther wrote about 35 hymns and is probably most famous for "A mighty fortress," sometimes called the Battle Hymn of the Reformation. Indeed, some of his hymns sound like doctrinal marches against the enemy. But I like to hope that were Luther asked which hymn best represents his deepest passion for the church, he would vote for "From heaven above." For before and after his efforts as ecclesiastical warrior, Luther was a teacher of the Bible, translating and preaching it so that all the assembly could hear and learn the word. Thus Luther wrote hymns, so that the people's backbone could be strengthened by biblical piety. Congregational song, he said, "drives away the devil and makes people cheerful."

In such a spirit, Luther wrote this Christmas ballad for his family of Katherine and six children, the last just newborn, in 1534. Two of our hymnals, one Roman Catholic and one Lutheran, include 14 of the stanzas: Why have a ballad if you omit ten of the verses? For the first stanza Luther rewrote a popular children's ring dance, changing a few of the words but retaining the spirit of sprightly fun. When several years later the hymn became popular for parish use, Luther composed the tune we now use, substituting it for the dance tune. But the spirit of children's play remained, and the easy scale patterns of the tune Vom Himmel Hoch must be sung quickly, lightly, playfully.

Like a medieval drama, the ballad gives some lines to an angelic messenger and the rest to the family of singers who come to the stable to worship. Although the ballad is childlike, it is not childish, but includes Luther's deepest theological convictions. The faithful will find not merely an infant but God's very self:

> In manger-bed, in swaddling clothes
> the child who all the earth upholds.

The prince in this manger has, instead of "velvets soft and silken stuff, . . . hay and straw so rough." Luther's medieval spirituality is popularized in stanzas like the following:

> O dearest Jesus, holy child,
> prepare a bed, soft, undefiled,
> a holy shrine, within my heart,
> that you and I need never part.

This is a good Luther to memorialize: not the Luther cussing out his opponents but the Luther singing the Bible with his family.

Let us find occasions to keep such ballads alive. Scholars have discovered that in ancient times the whole of the Iliad and all the exploits of Beowulf would have been sung aloud for communal enjoyment. Are we so atrophied that we can gasp out only two or three stanzas before we need a nap? Ten minutes several times a year spent in singing out every single stanza can be an enjoyable way to receive the word and call out, "Thanks be to God."

Jesus, Remember Me

Jesus, remember me
when you come into your kingdom.
Jesus, remember me,
when you come into your kingdom.

Jacques Berthier

Simple Gifts

Tis the gift to be simple, 'tis the gift to be free,
'tis the gift to come down where we ought to be,
and when we find ourselves in the place just right,
'twill be in the valley of love and delight.
When true simplicity is gained
to bow and to bend we shan't be ashamed,
to turn, turn, will be our delight,
till by turning, turning we come round right.

The Shakers

In the second of the two pivotal events at the weekly Christian assembly, we give thanks and eat and drink together as the body of Christ. Bread and wine are revealed to be the very body and blood of Christ; in sharing both the food and the revelation, we become that presence of Christ in the world. The event of communing in the bread and the cup and so becoming the body of Christ is both an instantaneous and a perpetual event; it happens mysteriously in the eating, it develops over the centuries. But practically speaking, the event takes about ten minutes, a good time to sing. In some parishes the seated worshipers maintain the song, while those processing, waiting and communing are silent. But other congregations seek songs appropriate for those actively communing. What is appropriate music to accompany walking, seeing one's place, eating, drinking, meditating, praying? One option is the song composed by Jacques Berthier.

An organist and composer from Paris, Jacques Berthier has collaborated with the Taizé community to provide music for their unique liturgical situation. Taizé, an ecumenical male monastic community near Cluny in France, has become a pilgrimage site at which sometimes thousands of people converge for the liturgy. Yet even when only a few dozen visitors join their assembly, the Taizé brothers sought liturgical song that was linguistically available to many language groups, that allowed everyone to be active participants in prayer, and that was musically worthy. Berthier offered his ostinato responses as one solution.

In these ostinato responses, a few well-chosen words allow the worshipers to enter into the depths of the Christian message without getting snarled in complicated syntax. The repetitive nature of the chants encourages active participation when people are walking about. Like any musical style, the Berthier chants can be deadly if poorly performed, if repeated mindlessly. But if sung creatively, they can be the vehicle for profound meditative prayer. The assembly can sing in four-part harmony. Soloists can add an obbligato. Instruments can provide interludes. Dynamics can vary. The numerous musical variations balance the utter simplicity of text.

One appropriate ostinato refrain for the communion is "Jesus, remember me." Here we take the place of the thief on the cross. Like the Jesus Prayer, the simple biblical quote means to unify the self, unite the self with the community and draw the assembly deeper and deeper into the mystery of redemption. The ebb and flow of the chant swims us up to communion and back to our seats, back to the crucifixion and up to the kingdom.

The Taizé community remains skeptical that celebrations in North America, utilizing varied musical styles, could benefit from the inclusion of just one Berthier chant. But here the brothers underestimate the power of their chant. The brothers hope for a spirit of recollection in the liturgy, and many Christians throughout the world, no matter what their musical styles, have discovered in Berthier's chants a matrix for just such recollection and in the communion the occasion for such recollection.

But perhaps a particular feast begs not for a meditative walk but for a spritely step, a connection not with male monastic solemnity but with American spiritedness. Fortunately we have such a chant in a Shaker song. Most famous since their demise for their artistic furnishings and their astonishing ingenuity, the Shakers—the United Society of Believers in Christ's Second Appearing—lived in farming communes throughout the American East and Midwest as one of our country's most successful utopian experiments. The Shakers believed that God, both masculine and feminine, was incarnate in both Jesus Christ and Mother Ann Lee, and that in celibate but sexually equal communities the believers were already living in the kingdom of God. Called Shakers because of their early ecstatic shaking, they developed stylized sex-segregated line dances as part of their worship meetings, and some of their unaffected songs accompanied their dancing before the Lord.

"'Tis the gift to be simple" is their most renowned song, the tune memorialized by Aaron Copland in his "Appalachian Spring" and reused in the problematic ballad "The Lord of the Dance." Probably composed for a Shaker revival in 1848, the text of "Simple Gifts" holds together the greatest paradox of the Christian life: It is when we "come down where we ought to be" that we are most free. As their dance moved through its figures, the worshipers bowing, bending and turning, the words affirmed that their final stopping place is "the valley of love and delight." Could we sing this song as we process, or perhaps skip, up to the table for communion? Could African American choirs teach everyone else how to sashay up to the altar?

"Jesus, remember me" and "'Tis the gift to be simple" seem more than a century apart, one the reverent prayer of twentieth-century postwar ecumenists, one the dance tune of nineteenth-century utopian sectarians. It is good that we need a number of communion songs annually. Sometimes we can pray with the men in the French countryside, sometimes we can dance with Mother Ann Lee's people in their meetinghouses. But the songs are also two of a kind: simple words and tunes sung by small groups of Christians, who by living in religious community anticipated the kingdom that they believe God will give. May their music grace our table.

THE YEAR

Advent
Christmastime

*...Now
he shines,
the long-
expected...*

"Of the Father's love
begotten,"
Aurelius Prudentius

O Come, O Come, Emmanuel

O come, O come, Emmanuel,
   and ransom captive Israel,
that mourns in lonely exile here
until the Son of God appear.
Rejoice! Rejoice! Emmanuel shall come to thee, O Israel!

O come, thou Wisdom from on high,
who orderest all things mightily;
to us the path of knowledge show,
and teach us in her ways to go.

O come, O come, thou Lord of might,
who to thy tribes on Sinai's height
in ancient times didst give the law,
in cloud, and majesty, and awe.

O come, thou Branch of Jesse's tree,
free them from Satan's tyranny
that trust thy mighty power to save,
and give them victory o'er the grave.

O come, thou Key of David, come,
and open wide our heavenly home;
make safe the way that leads on high,
and close the path to misery.

O come, thou Dayspring from on high,
and cheer us by thy drawing nigh;
disperse the gloomy clouds of night,
and death's dark shadow put to flight.

O come, Desire of nations, bind
all peoples in one heart and mind;
bid thou our sad divisions cease,
and be thyself our king of peace.

anon.

Christus Paradox

You, Lord, are both lamb and shepherd,
you, Lord, are both prince and slave,
you, peacemaker and sword-bringer
of the way you took and gave.
You, the everlasting instant,
you whom we both scorn and crave.

Clothed in light upon the mountain,
stripped of might upon the cross,
shining in eternal glory,
beggared by a soldier's toss.
You, the everlasting instant,
you who are our gift and cost.

You who walk each day beside us,
sit in power at God's side,
you who preach a way that's narrow
have a love that reaches wide.
You, the everlasting instant,
you who are our pilgrim guide.

Worthy is our earthly Jesus,
worthy is our cosmic Christ,
worthy your defeat and vict'ry,
worthy still your peace and strife.
You, the everlasting instant,
you who are our death and life.

Sylvia Dunstan

Shopping malls have discovered that Advent is marketable. Americans, even those with minimal religious conviction, will buy Advent wreaths and Advent calendars and Advent recipe books. But "Advent calendars" beginning with December 1 have more to do with shopping days until Christmas than with the four Sundays before the feast of the incarnation. Our consumer society thinks that what we anticipate during Advent is presents. Gifts, once a sign of God's presence, have for many people replaced God altogether.

Often our churches try to correct this image of mobbed malls and plastic Christmas trees by offering instead the image of a newborn. Mary's belly is growing, suggest clever Advent banners. Men preach about the glories of pregnancy, and crèche sets are ready and waiting for the baby doll to appear at the Midnight Mass. We understand something of childbirth, and we know something of how to anticipate it.

However, the church's deepest instinct has proclaimed that it is not a baby we anticipate; after all, the baby was born two millenia ago. Rather, we anticipate a re-created universe. When God comes, today, tomorrow, at the end of our time, the earth's terrain will be convulsed, the social hierarchy will topple, the subjugated young woman will be crowned queen. Such a rending of the heavens will be cataclysmic, even catastrophic for those high up on the mountain. We do not know what this coming of God will be like, but we are in awe of its promise.

These deeper intimations of joy coming for the whole world order enrich much of the church's classic Advent hymnody. Our great hymns focus not on a coming baby but on the coming Messiah. King, judge, liberator, savior, prince of peace are images inspired by the historic Hebrew hope that because utopia is imminent, we must live in anticipation of its arrival. Our Advent hymns call on God to be servant, light, sun, lamb, bridegroom. Charles Wesley's hymn "Come thou long-expected Jesus" uses abstract nouns to describe the coming one: rest, strength, consolation, hope, desire, joy.

The ninth-century monks, who spent their lives preparing themselves in the desert for the arrival of God, found in the Hebrew Scriptures seven concrete images for God's coming. In the seven days before Christmas they set off their daily chanting of the Magnificat with these antiphons of anticipation. When God arrives, and the world order is turned upside down, what will divinity be like? We have only images, partial pictures, but we use as many as we can.

The monks' "O antiphons" say that God's coming will be mighty Lady Wisdom residing in our land, dispensing justice along with bread and wine for the poor. God's coming will be the majestic appearance of the Lawgiver, without whose guidance there is chaos in the land. God's coming will be a Tree of Life blossoming full and bounteous from what had seemed only a moribund stump. God's coming will be the royal Key to open prisons, both the prisons in our life and the prison of the grave. On the solstice, the monks thought of the birthing sun and sang out that God's coming will be that very Solstice, that Newborn Day, that Rising Sun, enlightening a darkening world. God's coming will be Peace, the desire of every nation on earth. And finally, as Mary's Magnificat had tried to tell us, God will no longer maintain residence on the top of the mountain, but will dwell with, even within, us: Emmanuel. And then the whole world must be free, for where God is, no one can be bound.

During the twelfth century, a poet cast the "O antiphons" into Latin verse, and through a continuing tradition of translation we receive these antiphons as the hymn "O come, O come, Emmanuel." These seven images put into our Advent song the Jewish and Christian hope that God will indeed come to redeem the world. The images suggest to our minds a utopia far beyond Christmas gifts, a new world only begun in Jesus' birth. Our Christmas trees are Branches of Jesse in our homes, our year-end charity is Lady Wisdom re-creating the world, our gifts to one another are Keys unlocking all the doors we close throughout the year. Fortunately there is time to sing all seven stanzas; over and over during the communion is a possibility. The medieval chant helps join us with the history of longing, the ancient prophets and the medieval monks all praying for the coming joy.

These images are ageless in two ways. Like C. G. Jung's archetypes, the "O antiphons" outlast the centuries, recurring in every age and place. Symbols like the great wise woman, the old lawgiver, the tree of life and the sun connect us not only to Jewish and Christian hopes for salvation but to the whole religious world, with all its goddesses and gods and divinized nature. The "O antiphons" are primordial human prayer, the subterranean rivers of these archetypes nourishing even our modern assemblies. "O come, O come" is ageless also in its objectivity. The elevated Lady Wisdom is an image already open to the toddler, still open to the frail and forgetful. The bids in each stanza are metaphoric: "close the path to misery" is a petition that can have some meaning for everyone.

Seven images are better than one or two. Each image enlarges another, Lady Wisdom balancing Lawgiver, Dayspring illuminating Key. The danger of enshrining favorite images of God is that the fewer the images we use, even if they are biblical and orthodox, the more likely that either idolatry or silliness sets in. So we turn to poets and mystics to inspire us with yet more images. During these very weeks of Advent, we commemorate the death days of the Christian poets Ambrose, Thomas Merton and John of the Cross, whose words broaden and deepen our picture of the coming joy.

Another such poet is Sylvia Dunstan, a clergywoman in the United Church of Canada, who contributes to our Advent imagery the hymn "Christus Paradox." Dunstan's hymn invokes double-sided biblical images: lamb and shepherd, prince and slave. She recalls the theological paradoxes: Christ both walks each day beside us and sits in power at God's side. Poets call two adjacent contradictory words an oxymoron. Dunstan uses such an oxymoron: Her Christ is "the everlasting instant," more than we can know, more than our grammatically correct sentences can say. Like the "O antiphons," her images pour out and flow over, anticipating God's salvation. The stanzas ask for nothing: They merely name and praise the paradox, present and coming.

Let the plethora of images broaden and deepen our meager imaginations, opening our minds for a greater God. Then our shopping for gifts, far from replacing God, can be a sign of divine boundlessness, one gift for each image of God's perfection.

Good Christian Friends, Rejoice

ood Christian friends, rejoice
with heart and soul and voice;
give ye heed to what we say:
Jesus Christ is born today;
ox and ass before him bow,
and he is in the manger now.
Christ is born today!
Christ is born today!

Good Christian friends, rejoice
with heart and soul and voice;
now ye hear of endless bliss:
Jesus Christ was born for this!
He has opened heaven's door,
and we are blest forevermore.
Christ was born for this!
Christ was born for this!

Good Christian friends, rejoice
with heart and soul and voice;
now ye need not fear the grave;
Jesus Christ was born to save!

Calls you one and calls you all
to gain his everlasting hall.
Christ was born to save!
Christ was born to save!

anon., tr. John Mason Neale

Hark! The Herald Angels Sing

Hark! The herald angels sing,
"Glory to the newborn King!
Peace on earth, and mercy mild
God and sinners reconciled!"
Joyful, all you nations, rise,
join the triumph of the skies;
with the angelic host proclaim,
"Christ is born in Bethlehem!"
  Hark! The herald angels sing,
  "Glory to the newborn King!"

Christ, by highest heaven adored,
Christ, the everlasting Lord,
late in time behold him come,
offspring of the Virgin's womb.
Veiled in flesh the Godhead see:
hail the incarnate Deity,
pleased as man with us to dwell,
Jesus, our Emmanuel.

Hail the heaven-born Prince of Peace!
Hail the Sun of Righteousness!
Light and life to all he brings,
risen with healing in his wings.
Mild he lays his glory by,
born that we no more may die,
born to raise us from the earth,
born to give us second birth.

Charles Wesley

A historical study published in 1907 entitled *The Thirteenth, Greatest of Centuries* argued that the thirteenth century's theological magnitude and papal power was the height of Christendom. Whether we grimace or cheer at such an ecclesial view, we know that after the thirteenth century was over, a powerful lay spirit arose. For it was during the fourteenth century that Julian of Norwich recorded her visions and gave counsel to travelers, Catherine of Siena walked over Europe reprimanding the hierarchy, and dramatic presentations of scriptural readings got raucous enough to be booted out of the sanctuary and so evolved into the mystery plays. The medieval synthesis was cracking apart, the stately march of the clerical orders disrupted by the people's dance. The people wanted music livelier than plainsong, and so they used the melodies of their ring dances to sing of Jesus' birth, life and death.

These fourteenth-century ring dances gave birth to our Christmas carols. Still popular in Christian assemblies is one of the oldest of these carols, the fourteenth-century "Good Christian friends, rejoice." Here are all the characteristics of the Christmas carol: a lively dance tune, in a sprightly rhythm; a refrain to encourage all levels of the people's participation; and lyrics based on homey details in the life of Jesus. These carols, marked by popular religious feeling, are eons away from the theological stanzas Aquinas had penned the previous century. The prophetic ox and ass of Isaiah 1 become the docile animals of the humble stable. We can hear the peasants singing of "endless bliss" and see them dancing at the possibility of gaining entrance into the lord's "everlasting hall." There is a wonderful legend concerning the origin of this carol: A fourteenth-century writer states that Heinrich Suso, a mystic who died in 1366, had a vision of angels drawing him into a dance and singing this carol to him, after which he sang it to us all.

The earliest carols were quite modern by being bilingual, usually having the stanzas in the vernacular and the refrain in Latin. Some of our carols retain this feeling: "Let our gladness have no end," a fifteenth-century Bohemian carol; "The first noel," a seventeenth-century English carol; "Angels we have heard on high," an eighteenth-century French carol; "The snow lay on the ground," a nineteenth-century Irish carol. Along with a dozen carol-like hymns, these carols remain the most popular Christmas hymns in our culture. We know them from loudspeakers at the department store, subliminally urging us to spend money for gifts. But let us not be too grouchy about this: Carols have always been popular songs outside the liturgy. The challenge for our assemblies is to sing these carols when they are appropriate— from Christmas Eve through Epiphany and the Baptism of the Lord—and so mark the season of Christmas.

The spirit of carols has shaped other Christmas hymns, even those written by famous authors known for their individual style. Among the preeminent Christian hymn-writers is Charles Wesley. An eighteenth-century Anglican, Charles Wesley and his brother John developed "methods" of spiritual exercises while students at Oxford, and the brothers spent their lives in itinerant preaching to those who came to be called Methodists. But along the way, Wesley visited among the Moravians, Christians famous to this day for their German hymn singing, and inspired by the dynamism of their congregational song, Wesley composed over 6,000 hymns for his Methodist Anglicans. It is awesome to realize that he composed at a rate of two and a half hymns a week for 50 years. About a dozen of his hymns remain ecumenically popular today.

Wesley's great Christmas hymn originally had ten four-line stanzas begining "Hark, how all the welkin rings," the welkin being the firmament in which God resides. Wesley included Pauline stanzas like the following:

Adam's likeness, Lord, efface,
stamp thy image in its place,
second Adam from above,
reinstate us in thy love.

But within three years of Wesley's death, the hymn was reshaped by the tradition of carols to become our "Hark! the herald angels sing" with its dance-like refrain. Carols have so formed Christians' Christmas imagination that if a Christmas hymn is not a carol, we will try to make it one. It is similar with the tune: Originally part of a concert piece composed by Felix Mendelssohn to honor Gutenberg and the printing press, the melody was reshaped to express the people's joyous Christmas celebration. Let this hymn be a lesson to liturgical purists: Centuries of worshiping Christians can turn even artistic genius into excellent liturgy.

Because of their accessible syntax, Wesley's hymns sound far simpler than they are. "Hark! the herald angels sing" includes theological ideas like "the incarnate deity" and biblical references like Malachi's "healing in his wings." Wesley applied his genius throughout the liturgical year. From him we have "Come, thou long-expected Jesus," "Christ the Lord is risen today," "Hail the day that sees him rise," and "Rejoice, the Lord is King." He knew the scriptures, he had studied theology, he honored the church year, and he wrote verse both straightforward and profound.

We cannot leave Charles Wesley's contribution to hymnody without reading again his brother John's 1761 "Directions for Singing," instructions to the Methodist Anglicans to ensure lively song. "Beware of singing as if you were half dead, or half asleep; but lift up your voice with strength. Be no more afraid of your voice now, nor more ashamed of its being heard, than when you sung the songs of Satan." The Wesleys knew the spirit of the ring dance; they hoped that people would apply the liveliness of secular song to the church's praise. I think we succeed at least at Christmastime, when sprightly songs, if not ring dances, still mark corporate worship. With carols like "Good Christian friends, rejoice" and "Hark! the herald angels sing," the assembly's song at least on Christmas Day will not be half dead.

O Morning Star, How Fair and Bright

O Morning Star, how fair and bright!
  You shine with God's own truth and light,
aglow with grace and mercy.
Of Jacob's race, King David's Son,
our Lord and master, you have won
our hearts to serve you only!
Lowly, holy!
Great and glorious,
all victorious,
rich in blessing!
Rule and might o'er all possessing.

Come, heavenly bridegroom, light divine,
and deep within our hearts now shine;
there light a flame undying.
In your one body let us be
as living branches of a tree,
your life our lives supplying.

Now, though daily
earth's deep sadness
may perplex us
and distress us,
yet with heavenly joy you bless us.

Lord, when you look on us in love,
at once there falls from God above
a ray of purest pleasure.
Your Word and Spirit, flesh and blood
refresh our souls with heavenly food.
You are our dearest treasure!
Let your mercy
warm and cheer us!
Oh, draw near us!
For you teach us
God's own love through you has reached us.

Oh, let the harps break forth in sound!
Our joy be all with music crowned,
our voices gaily blending!

For Christ goes with us all the way—
today, tomorrow, ev'ry day!
his love is never ending!
Sing out! Ring out!
Jubilation!
Exultation!
Tell the story!
Great is he, the King of glory!

Philipp Nicolai, tr. composite

Wake, O Wake

Wake, O wake, and sleep no longer,
　　for he who calls you is no stranger:
awake, God's own Jerusalem!
Hear, the midnight bells are chiming
the signal for his royal coming:
let voice to voice announce his name!
We feel his footsteps near,
the Bridegroom at the door—
Alleluia!
The lamps will shine
with light divine
as Christ the savior comes to reign.

Zion hears the sound of singing;
our hearts are thrilled with sudden longing:
she stirs, and wakes, and stands prepared.
Christ, her friend, and lord, and lover,
her star and sun and strong redeemer—
at last his mighty voice is heard.
The Son of God has come
to make with us his home:
sing Hosanna!

The fight is won,
the feast begun:
we fix our eyes on Christ alone.

Glory, glory, sing the angels,
while music sounds from strings and cymbals;
all humankind, with songs arise!
Twelve the gates into the city,
each one a pearl of shining beauty;
the streets of gold ring out with praise.
All creatures round the throne
adore the holy One
with rejoicing:
Amen be sung
by ev'ry tongue
to crown their welcome to the King.

Philipp Nicolai, tr. Christopher Idle

Martin Luther was passionately concerned that the liturgy be the praise of the people, not the task of the priest. Being not only a biblical scholar but a musician as well, he sought to provide a body of hymns for the people's liturgical participation. Like the medieval meistersingers, he and his followers wrote both the tunes and the lyrics for their chorales. It is important to realize that the chorales were not extraneous music or choir anthems; chorale is the German word for Gregorian chant. These chorales included both the ordinary of the liturgy and "the hymn of the day." Still today many Lutherans cannot imagine an entirely spoken liturgy, and when Lutherans ask what is the liturgy of the day, they are inquiring which is the appointed musical setting.

The early Reformation hymns were corporate confessions of faith. Whether a Gloria, a Christianized psalm or a blast of Reformation doctrine, these hymns were objective communal creeds. Melodies were vigorous, rhythms were syncopated. But this objectivity in Lutheran hymnody ran its course, and by the seventeenth century yielded to personal devotion. We call Pietism the movement that gave us German chorales composed to be the proper "hymn of the day" but focusing on the pious emotions of the individual believer. At this historical juncture, when Reformation creed met personal pietism, stands one of the church's premier hymns, called since the nineteenth century the Queen of Chorales.

Philipp Nicolai was a Lutheran pastor living in the second half of the sixteenth century. A product of the universities of Erfurt and Wittenberg, he was renowned both for preaching like Chrysostom and for attacking Calvinists with virulent polemics. He is remembered, however, not for such stereotypical Lutheran spirit, but for the two love songs he composed. Communal tragedy inspired him to write: In 1597–1598 the plague killed 1,300 of his parishioners, and he wrote some meditations and hymns, as his preface says, "to leave behind me (if God should call me from this world) as the token of my peaceful, joyful, Christian departure, or (if God should spare me in health) to comfort other sufferers whom he should also visit with the pestilence." One morning he sat down to write. He forgot to eat lunch, and by three o'clock in the afternoon had completed the seven stanzas of "Wie schön leuchtet."

Our hymnals offer different translations: "O Morning Star, how fair and bright" and "How bright appears the Morning Star" are two current renditions. Using medieval monastic tradition, Nicolai based his Christian meditation on Psalm 45, the wedding song of the queen and the king, and he described his hymn as "a spiritual bridal song of the believing soul concerning Jesus Christ, her heavenly bridegroom." In his love song he memorialized his 15-year-old theological student, whose initials of name and title form the acrostic (W E G U H Z W) of the opening words of each stanza. The hymn contains the poignant glimpse of a man's devotion to his student, who died in the plague, hidden within his many-faceted adoration of God. Warm and affectionate, the text sings out the passion of the faithful believer. The German verse, although clearly a congregational hymn, is cast in the first personal singular, creating an interesting paradox between the "we" of the church and the "I" of the believer that modern translations have abandoned.

The hymn contains a wealth of Epiphany imagery. In some of our churches, Epiphany is a single feast day, perhaps a Sunday; in other churches it is a season in which to explore images of the presence of God in Jesus' ministry. At Epiphany, God enlightens the world with the shining Christ, and in that light God in love is wed to the whole world. Nicolai opens his love song with the image of Christ as the morning star shining brightly. Succeeding stanzas—we must sing more than three!—include images of Christ as king, bridegroom, tree, food, treasure, ransom, the first and the last. Because of Nicolai's reliance on biblical imagery, the praise is not privately the author's: In classic Lutheran tradition, it is the people's hymn of Epiphany. It is biblical creed and personal devotion illumining our Epiphany celebrations.

The hymn is constructed brilliantly. In the first half of each long stanza, the rhythm is iambic: short-LONG, short-LONG, "o MORNing STAR, how FAIR and BRIGHT." The tune Nicolai composed for this first half climbs up the octave. Then comes the "Amen, Amen" hinge, repeated stressed syllables called spondees. The second half of each stanza is written in trochees, LONG-short, LONG-short, "GREAT and GLORious, ALL vic-TORious." Meanwhile the tune descends the octave from top to bottom. The hymn, text and tune, becomes a graceful arch, a rise and fall, constructed in one day. It is the Queen.

Nicolai's second masterpiece, "Wake, O wake," is another love song. Three stanzas long, forming another acrostic on his student Wilhelm's name, the hymn inter-weaves the parable of the wise and foolish bridesmaids with images from the Book of Revelation about heaven's joys. Nicolai's lectionary, and ours until the recent reforms, read the Matthew 25 parable of the wise and foolish bridesmaids during Advent. However, modern hymnals need not continue assigning this hymn to Advent. "Wake, O wake" is one of the church's most vigorous hymns about life with God. Christopher Idle's translation is superb, even to retaining the student's initials, W Z G, to head the stanzas. Such strong rather than sappy images help us to celebrate eucharistic union and perhaps even believe in heaven once again.

"Wake, O wake" has been called the King of Chorales. But in this monarchy, the Queen reigns supreme.

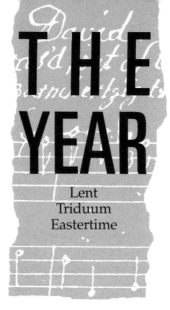

THE YEAR

Lent
Triduum
Eastertime

. . . What language shall I borrow . . .

"O sacred head, now wounded,"
Paul Gerhardt

The Glory of These Forty Days

The glory of these forty days
we celebrate with songs of praise;
for Christ, by whom all things were made,
himself has fasted and has prayed.

Alone and fasting Moses saw
the loving God who gave the law;
and to Elijah, fasting, came
the steeds and chariots of flame.

So Daniel trained his mystic sight,
delivered from the lion's might;
and John, the Bridegroom's friend, became
the herald of Messiah's name.

Then grant that we like them be true,
consumed in fast and prayer with you;
our spirits strengthen with your grace,
and give us joy to see your face.

asc. Gregory, tr. Maurice Bell

Jesus, Your Blood and Righteousness

Jesus, your blood and righteousness
  my beauty are, my glorious dress;
'mid flaming worlds, in these arrayed,
with joy shall I lift up my head.

Bold shall I stand in that great day,
cleansed and redeemed, no debt to pay;
for by your cross, absolved I am
from sin and guilt, from fear and shame.

Lord, I believe your precious blood,
which at the mercy-seat of God
pleads for the captives' liberty,
was also shed in love for me.

When from the dust of death I rise
to claim my mansion in the skies,
this then shall be my only plea:
Christ Jesus lived and died for me.

Then shall I praise you and adore
your blessed name forevermore,
who once, for me and all you made,
an everlasting ransom paid.

Nicolaus L. von Zinzendorf, tr. John Wesley, alt.

The revised liturgical calendar gives to the whole of Lent a baptismal and a communal character it has not had for centuries. Gone is the self-flagellating Way of the Cross we associate with this season. Our hymnals have been purged of many late medieval expressions of Lenten personal penance. For example, recent hymnals that print Isaac Watts's "Alas! and did my Savior bleed" have altered the line "for such a worm as I" to "for sinners such as I." I-as-a-worm has met both Christian roots and the human potential movement and has emerged as the community-as-pilgrim.

From Ash Wednesday on, we are to think of the newly excavated baptistry in which Augustine was baptized by Ambrose, a great circular space in which the individual was embraced by the community. Ash Wednesday's readings preface Matthew's call to fasting, prayer and almsgiving with Joel's promise of grain, wine and oil for the whole community. Roman Catholics have been offered alternative ritual words at the imposition of ashes: Turn away from sin and be faithful to the gospel. Private penance is turned toward communal life.

Thus Ash Wednesday poses a conundrum, because baptism into the community is not why believers flock to the liturgy on Ash Wednesday. Our willing donning of ashes is a powerful symbol of the pervasive Western belief that I am at fault. Oedipus, seeking the culprit, discovers that it is he. Hebrew prophets and Christian saints point to the individual as the locus of sin and death. Not the Milan baptistry but Augustine's relentless confessions hold the key to our self-reflective consciousness. The ritual of receiving ashes is far more individually focused than that of taking communion. "The body of Christ" intends, although English obscures this fact, a plural you: the body of Christ is for the community. But "Remember, O woman, that you are dust, and to dust you shall return" addresses the individual believer, marked now with ashes as by sin and death.

We encounter a liturgical paradox. Countless Christians cram the churches on Ash Wednesday to ritualize their private penance. But there they meet a pre-medieval, thus alien, spirit, asking them to join with others in baptism. The event is at odds with itself. Thus choosing hymns for this liturgy is difficult. Hymnals do not appoint hymns specifically for Ash Wednesday, and traditional hymns expressing personal penance tend to be so lugubrious that they are counterproductive of a new Lent.

Perhaps the most appropriate classic hymn for Ash Wednesday is "The glory of these forty days." This sixth-century text rides the paradox of the day admirably. "The glory of these forty days we celebrate with songs of praise." Here the penance of the days in the wilderness meets the community's praise for forgiveness. The text refers to the stories of Moses, Elijah, Daniel, John the baptizer and Christ. Rather than being alone in our confession, we stand with these faithful witnesses who were "consumed in fast and prayer with you." The closing reference to our joy at finally seeing the face of God is especially appropriate on the day that we mar our human faces with the ashes of our shame and mortality.

The hymn is ascribed to Gregory the Great, who as a nobleman, became prefect of Rome and as an ascetic, contributed his considerable wealth to establish six Benedictine monasteries. As pope, he worked to simplify the liturgy, which was becoming ever more complex and clerical. Legend gives his name to the plainsong that developed in the reorganized Schola Cantorum. Gregorian chant itself became complex and clerical, but that was hardly Gregory's fault. However, scholars debate whether "Clarum decus ieiunii," "The glory of these forty days," was penned by Gregory himself. We are at least safe in asserting that it was Gregory-inspired, articulating an early Benedictine spirituality that was both ascetic and communal. Thus in singing this hymn on Ash Wednesday we don something of Gregory's spirituality, quite appropriate for a new Lent.

A second hymn of the day is even harder to locate. Of all the Christians who sang about personal penance, the Moravians seemed best able to do so with a cheerful heart. Yet their hymns are being lost to Christians outside their community, and the denomination is known only for its many-pointed Christmas stars hanging in windows and lighting up porches. But the Moravian story is worth remembering, and a hymn or two suggested.

The story begins in the fourteenth century, when the Roman Catholic priest John Hus in what is now southern Germany was burned at the stake for first pressing Reformation concerns. A community of his followers survived as the Bohemian Brethren. In the seventeenth century, this group took refuge on the lands of a Lutheran count named Nicolaus von Zinzendorf, who eventually became their bishop and led these Moravian Brethren all over the world with a charism for missionary work. Count Zinzendorf led them singing. He wrote over 2,000 hymns—his Christmas hymn was 37 stanzas long—which because of their excessive emotionalism are largely forgotten today. But his spirit birthed much of the church's hymnody. For example, it was visiting Zinzendorf and marveling at the Moravians' singing that inspired Charles Wesley to begin writing hymns.

Zinzendorf's hymn "Jesus, your blood and righteousness" is appropriate for Ash Wednesday. The hymn moves the focus from the individual to the community, from the "I" with joyfully uplifted head to "all you made." The references to the bodily stance and dress of the believer sound as if Zinzendorf had the Ash Wednesday ritual in mind. Yet the hymn is marked by the joy of the believer: "bold shall I stand in that great day." "When from the dust of death I rise, to claim my mansion in the skies," the believer will sing lustily of gratitude to Christ. The hymn turns personal penance into communal praise. A lively long-meter tune can be selected.

Zinzendorf's passion for dynamic hymnody inspired his follower James Montgomery, the author of "Angels we have heard on high." He wrote 400 hymns, of which perhaps half a dozen are sung in our century. Montgomery began as a Moravian missionary, but most of his years he was an editor and prolific poet. His hymn "Come to Calvary's holy mountain" calls all who "come in sorrow and contrition" to the pure and healing fountain, the soul-renewing flood. The text enlivens all sinners "ruined by the fall" with communal baptismal imagery and is highly appropriate for Ash Wednesday.

Contemporary hymnwriters, please bend your art to Ash Wednesday. It is a challenge, to honor the people's millennium-long personal penance while transforming it into the start of the community's pilgrimage. We die individually, but we live together: Can we sing these both? Many psalms express personal lament turned to communal praise. Perhaps we can learn from our own past an appropriate song for Ash Wednesday.

O Jesus, Joy of Living Hearts

O Jesus, joy of loving hearts,
   the fount of life and our true light,
we seek the peace your love imparts
and stand rejoicing in your sight.

Your truth unchanged has ever stood;
you save all those who heed your call;
to those who seek you, you are good,
to those who find you all in all.

We taste you, Lord, our living bread,
and long to feast upon you still;
we drink of you, the fountainhead,
our thirsting souls to quench and fill.

For you our restless spirits yearn
where'er our changing lot is cast;
glad, when your presence we discern,
blest, when our faith can hold you fast.

O Jesus, ever with us stay;
make all our moments calm and bright;
oh, chase the night of sin away,
shed o'er the world your holy light.

asc. Bernard of Clairvaux, tr. Ray Palmer, alt.

What Wondrous Love

What wondrous love is this, O my soul, O my soul!
What wondrous love is this, O my soul!
What wondrous love is this
that caused the Lord of bliss
to bear the dreadful curse for my soul, for my soul,
to bear the dreadful curse for my soul?

When I was sinking down, sinking down, sinking down,
when I was sinking down, sinking down,
when I was sinking down
beneath God's righteous frown
Christ laid aside his crown for my soul, for my soul,
Christ laid aside his crown for my soul.

To God and to the Lamb I will sing, I will sing;
to God and to the Lamb I will sing;
to God and to the Lamb
who is the great I AM,
while millions join the theme, I will sing, I will sing,
while millions join the theme, I will sing.

And when from death I'm free, I'll sing on, I'll sing on;
and when from death I'm free, I'll sing on;
and when from death I'm free,
I'll sing and joyful be,
and through eternity I'll sing on, I'll sing on,
and through eternity I'll sing on.

anon.

Because centuries of Lenten penance were so successful, the dilemma of Ash Wednesday continues throughout the Lenten season. Westerners are adept at introspection: One could argue that the Enlightenment and the therapeutic movement are secular offspring of such self-examination. Droves of Christians give up this or that trifle in sincere desire to demonstrate their interior devotion. Meanwhile Sunday morning, always a celebration of Christ's resurrection, points us toward Easter and calls individual penitents into community. By forming a circle around the font, we come to constitute the community, and as a community, we become what we receive, the body of Christ.

In many congregations, one hymn each Sunday is chosen to complement the readings. But during Lent, for a second hymn during the liturgy, we might well sing one of the classic hymns in which the community meditates on the meaning of Christ. Rather than morbid attention to the passion that we know from the recent past, these hymns can be invigorating anamnesis, hymns that celebrate Christ's Spirit alive in the sacramental community, songs to praise God alive in the baptized.

An excellent hymn for this purpose is "O Jesus, joy of loving hearts." Popular in the United States in the nineteenth-century translation by Ray Palmer, the hymn is a rendition of five stanzas of the 42-stanza, twelfth-century Latin poem "Jesu dulcis memoria." In this poem the community seeks Christ, finds Christ, but seeks yet more:

We taste you, everliving bread,
and long to feast upon you still.

The poem articulates the community's devotion to Christ: "Our restless spirits yearn" for life. The poem's last line anticipates the coming light of the Easter vigil: "shed o'er the world your holy light."

Tradition ascribes this poem to the mystic Bernard of Clairvaux, the skeletally thin ascetic abbot who was perhaps the most powerful Western man alive—surely the most influential religious force—in the early twelfth century. He is venerated as the force behind the Cistercian order, a rigorous reform movement within Benedictine monasticism. Bernard believed that plain walls, unadorned capitals, clear glass and a merciless house-cleaning of images would create the simplicity required for Christian contemplation and that radical silence in the community would free the tongue for praise. As well, with comments that shock even the male chauvinists among us, he was adamantly opposed to any contact of his monks with women. But, exhibiting the familiar pattern of refusing love-talk to human beings only to address it to God, his love poems to Christ and to the Virgin are among the most lush in the Christian tradition.

We do not know whether "Jesu dulcis memoria" was the work of Bernard, but scholars agree it was the product of some great twelfth-century Cistercian poet. For although Cistercian church edifices were barren of ornament, although the monks kept austere silence in their communities, and although they expressed disgust at even the idea of sexual contact, their spirituality let all these guards down when adoring Christ. Their eloquent sermons and poems were thickly metaphorical; they praised communally; and they fell deeply in love with the divine.

The stanzas that have become "O Jesus, joy of loving hearts" are generally sung to the waltz tune Walton. The hymn is a courting song, a beckoning song of a love made stronger because the lovers are already married. Let us sing it as a lively waltz, our spirits if not our bodies dancing with God. The hymn is rare in that while it is based on the medieval metaphor of the lover, it is devoid of gender-specific language. Cast in the second person, the words praise "you," not he. We can sing of sexual union with God without the perennial problem that the divine gets assigned the masculine dynamism and the human a feminine submissiveness. Perhaps because Bernard taught his Cistercians to believe that human free will cooperates with divine grace, this poem is more likely than those of other spiritualities to cast the two lovers as parallel partners.

The theme of our devotion to God through Christ takes on more rugged expression in the anonymous nineteenth-century American hymn "What wondrous love is this." First appearing in an 1811 collection, this folk hymn was included in the ground-breaking hymnal *Southern Harmony*. First published in Philadelphia in 1835, this remarkable collection sold 600,000 copies in the nineteenth century and is still used by songsters in Appalachia. This popularly revived hymn exemplies the best of the American gospel tradition.

The story goes that two brothers-in-law assembled the original collection, but that when the hymnal appeared in print, only the man who had traveled north to secure publication, William Walker, had his name on it. The family rift was never healed, and the other brother-in-law published another famous hymnal, *Sacred Harp*. But from the agonies of one family came riches for American Protestantism. *Southern Harmony*'s 334 hymns exhibited a wide variety of text and tune, and it met a dire need for better singing in American churches.

Already in the eighteenth century, Protestant clergy were bemoaning the decline of hymn singing. The spirit of the Reformation was aging, the homogeneity of communities dissolving. Thus about the time of the American Revolution, singing masters traveled from town to town presenting evening singing schools, teaching both the fundamentals of music and excellence in hymn-singing. A Philadelphian developed a technique of drawing different geometric shapes for the notes, to help people recognize the change of pitch. William Walker used this "shape note" technique in his *Southern Harmony,* and the success of the hymns went hand in hand with the popularity of shape-note notation.

Southern Harmony provides us a fascinating visit to nineteenth-century Protestantism. Walker's introduction

on the rudiments of music includes such advice as
"A frequent use of some acid drink, such as purified
cider, vinegar, and water mixed and sweetened with a little honey, or sugar with a little black or cayenne pepper,
wine, and loaf sugar, if used sparingly, are very strength-
ening to the lungs." Hymn #18 seems made for dis-
couraged church leaders:

> I am a great complainer, that bears the name of Christ:
> Come, all ye Zion mourners, and listen to my cries;
> I've many sore temptations, and sorrows to my soul;
> I feel my faith declining, and my affections cold.

Hymn #82, "The Romish Lady," is a ballad for eager
Protestants which narrates the gruesome details of
the pope's martyring a lady who would "no more pros-
trate herself to pictures decked with gold." Ecumen-
icity was a low priority during those days!

Hymn #252, "What wondrous love," is characterized
by frontier simplicity, repeated phrases and strong melody. When Appalachian folk sing such a hymn, the
melody is carried by the tenors and the altos; sopranos
and bass contribute a higher and a lower line of harmony. The resulting sound is extremely distinctive, its
scale and chords sounding primitive. Appalachian Christians sing this hymn very rapidly, about four times faster
than it is sometimes sung: the beat belongs not to the
quarter note but to the whole note, more a dance than a
dirge. Although the poem is cast in the singular, the
hymn is obviously a communal song rendered by the
entire assembly, millions joining the theme. Though
we may sink down on our own, we sing on together. The
words fit well a renewed Lent. The references to "the
dreadful curse" and "God's righteous frown" turn to praise
for divine love and the promise of heaven. Another fea-
ture commends it for our use: its nongender-specific
imagery of God.

In reviewing hymns about devotion to Christ, we think
also of Johann Franck's "Jesus, priceless treasure," made
beloved through J. S. Bach's cantata "Jesu, meine Freude."

But its words are more private than those of "Jesu dulcis memoria," its tune without the communal sense of *Southern Harmony*. As we move from Ash Wednesday to the Triduum, let us join not only one another but also the ghost of a medieval mystic and the spirit of the Appalachian pioneer. Such singing helps make a good Lent.

All Glory, Laud, and Honor

All glory, laud, and honor
to thee, Redeemer, King!
To whom the lips of children
made sweet hosannas ring.

Thou art the King of Israel,
thou David's royal Son,
who in the Lord's name comest,
the King and Blessed One.

The company of angels
are praising thee on high,
and we with all creation
in chorus make reply.

The people of the Hebrews
with psalms before thee went;
our prayer and praise and anthems
before thee we present.

To thee, before thy passion,
they sang their hymns of praise;
to thee, now high exalted,
our melody we raise.

Thou didst accept their praises;
accept the prayers we bring,
who in all good delightest,
thou good and gracious King.

Theodulph of Orleans, tr. John Mason Neale, alt.

Godhead Here Is Hiding

Godhead here is hiding whom I do adore
masked by these bare shadows, shape and nothing more,
see, Lord, at thy service low lies here a heart
lost, all lost in wonder at the God thou art.

Seeing, touching, tasting are in thee deceived;
how says trusty hearing? that shall be believed;
what God's Son has told me, take for truth I do;
truth himself speaks truly or there's nothing true.

On the cross thy Godhead made no sign to men;
here thy very manhood steals from human ken:
both are my confessions, both are my belief,
and I pray the prayer of the dying thief.

I am not Thomas, wounds I cannot see,
but I plainly call thee Lord and God as he:
this faith each day deeper by my holding of,
daily make me harder hope and dearer love.

O thou, our reminder of the Crucified,
living Bread, the life of us for whom he died,
lend this life to me, then; feed and feast my mind,
there by thou the sweetness I was meant to find.

Like what tender tales tell of the Pelican,
bathe me, Jesus Lord, in what thy bosom ran
blood that but one drop of has the power to win
all the world forgiveness of its world of sin.

Jesus, whom I look at shrouded here below,
I beseech thee, send me what I thirst for so,
some day to gaze on thee face to face in light
and be blest forever with thy glory's sight.

Thomas Aquinas, tr. Gerard M. Hopkins

People proud of their cause love a procession. Whether an emperor's victory march through the streets with prisoners shackled for display, or the annual Mummers Parade, at which in spite of below freezing temperatures some thousands of Philadelphians dress up in bizarre costumes and strut down Broad Street on New Year's Day, a procession is exhilarating both for the participants and the observers. The symbolic movement channels the people into their single cause. The parade moves our bodies with our minds, uniting ourselves with all the others.

Processions last for centuries. When Christian missionaries first arrived in northern Europe, they recorded their horror at watching the planting processions, in which the farmers marched through the newly plowed fields carrying a statue of the earth goddess, the men petitioning her to bless the fields with her fertility, the women dancing and singing her praises. But we are hardly surprised to discover that several centuries later bishops are leading those same processions, the beneficent goddess now a statue of Mary, the fertility prayers Christianized, the dancing women replaced by processing choirboys.

Egeria, a Christian pilgrim, wrote about her experience of the fourth-century palm procession. Here the archetypal urge to make symbolic procession gains yet more power, for the pilgrims have located their sacred site; they are encircling their axis mundi. Egeria describes the Christians processing through Jerusalem on the anniversary Sunday of Jesus' identical walk:

> Everyone walks down from the top of the Mount of Olives, with the people preceding the bishop and responding continually with "Blessed is he who comes in the name of the Lord" to the hymns and antiphons. All the children who are present here, including those who are not yet able to walk because they are too young, and therefore are carried on their parents' shoulders, all of them bear branches, some carrying palms, others olive branches. . . . Everyone accompanies the bishop the whole way on foot, and this includes distinguished ladies and men of consequence, reciting the responses all the while.

Egeria was much taken by the procession, as are we.

These days we may bemoan that modern people can't walk and sing at the same time. But our great civil rights marches proved it possible, even powerful, in our times. The Jerusalem palm procession became so popular in Christendom that it was exported throughout the world, for Christians believe that the axis mundi is not only the city of Jerusalem but any human space marked by the assembly, the word and the sacraments. So on Passion Sunday we at least attempt this age-old procession, walking about the church edifice or moving from one building to another or parading around the block, waving palm branches, remembering Egeria, remembering Christ, heading for the Triduum.

The hymn for the palm procession is "All glory, laud, and honor." The refrain, repeated praise of Christ, makes for easy participation, the tune a simple scale up and back. In the verses, we join with Jerusalem's children, the heavenly angels, the centuries of pilgrims and one another to enact our walk with Christ. The text is quite simply a description of the procession we are conducting. The hymn is over a millenium old. In the eighth century, Theodulph was made bishop of Orleans by Charlemagne, but later he was imprisoned for suspected political machinations. Legend has it that in 821 on Palm Sunday, Theodulph sang out this hymn from his prison cell as the palm procession moved through the streets. Even if not factual, the legend calls us to Christian truth: Our freedom marches next to the prison, the victorious march of Jesus anticipates his coming trial. Even the tune, now entitled St. Theodulph, symbolizes the ambivalency of the day: The strong and solid tune was first used as a lament for the dead during one of the seventeenth-century plagues. Theodulph's now suppressed final stanza is clever. The Latin reads: *Sis pius ascensor, tuus et nos simus asellus.* We plead with Christ to ride on us, for we are only the ass walking into the holy city.

It is appropriate that modern Christians use the translation crafted by John Mason Neale. Neale was an Anglican priest who because of his taste for elaborate liturgy was out of favor with his hierarchy and was relegated to meager ministerial positions. But he did not mope his days away. Able to read, write and think in 21 different languages, he spent his life's energies translating into English the classic Latin and Greek hymns of the early and medieval church. It is astonishing to realize how many of the church's beloved hymns were buried in ancient languages before Neale resurrected them for congregational song. There is Neale, practically imprisoned, and Theodulph, quite imprisoned, and Jesus walking toward prison, and we recall W. H. Auden:

Follow, poet, follow right
To the bottom of the night,
With your unconstraining voice
Still persuade us to rejoice;

In the deserts of the heart
Let the healing fountain start,
In the prison of his days
Teach the free man how to praise.

Could we simultaneously sing and process twice on one Sunday? For the communion there is Thomas Aquinas's hymn of eucharistic adoration, "Adoro te devote." Probably composed about 1260 at the request of the pope to prepare material for the newly appointed Corpus Christi procession, the hymn expresses Aquinas's complex eucharistic theology in accessible imagery. In successive stanzas Aquinas honors God hidden in symbols, praises Christ as truth, identifies with the dying thief and with doubting Thomas, likens Christ to bread and to the pelican, and cites the Pauline hope that finally we will see God face to face, without the symbolic veil. The poem is a brilliant piece of personal devotion on the redemptive meaning of the sacrament.

The hymn is notoriously difficult to render in modern English. Our hymnals offer "Thee we adore," "God with hidden majesty," "Humbly we adore thee" and "Godhead here is hiding." This last is not ideal, but it is the only contemporary translation that includes the sixth stanza, in which Christ is directly addressed as the merciful pelican, the mother who cuts open her breast to feed her children with her blood. A classic feminine image of divine love, the pelican legend deserves a place in our books. One parish sings during the communion a Taizé-like mantra based on this hymn by Aquinas:

> You we adore, O hidden Savior,
> You we adore, O hidden Savior.
> We are gathered like the wheat, one body in the bread,
> Bread of life, O Lord, shine forth, through whom we are fed.

The chant, reminiscent of the full poem, brings us not so much the scholarly Thomas of the *Summa Theologia,* but the mystic Thomas, who coming away from presiding at the eucharist one day said, "All that I have written is but straw compared with what I have just seen," and from that day on neither wrote nor dictated another word.

On Ash Wednesday we began, as Luther says, to creep back to our baptism. On Passion Sunday we process together, awash in the story of our victorious defeat. The spirit of our march comes to rest in the agony of the passion. It is hard to sit through such multivalence: It is a good day to process.

Where True Love and Charity Are Found

Where true love and charity are found, God is always there.
Ubi caritas et amor Deus ibi est.

Since the love of Christ has brought us all together,
let us all rejoice and be glad, now and always.
Let everyone love the Lord God, the living God;
and with sincere hearts let us love each other now.

Therefore when we gather as one in Christ Jesus,
let our love enfold each race, creed, every person.
Let envy, division and strife cease among us;
may Christ our Lord dwell among us in every heart.

Bring us with your saints to behold your great beauty,
there to see you, Christ our God, throned in great glory;
there to possess heaven's peace and joy, your truth and love,
for endless ages of ages, world without end.

anon., adp. Richard Proulx

Jesu, Jesu, Fill Us with Your Love

Jesu, Jesu, fill us with your love,
show us how to serve the neighbors we have from you.

Kneels at the feet of his friends,
silently washes their feet,
Master who acts as a slave to them.

Neighbors are rich and poor,
neighbors are black and white,
neighbors are near and far away.

These are the ones we should serve,
these are the ones we should love;
all these are neighbors to us and you.

Loving puts us on our knees,
serving as though we are slaves,
this is the way we should live with you.

Kneel at the feet of our friends,
silently washing their feet,
this is the way we should live with you.

Tom Colvin

We begin the Triduum on the Thursday which some call Holy, others Maundy. In the Eastern church the focus is on the betrayal by Judas; much of the Holy Week liturgy in the East is dramatization of the events in Jesus' last days. But the liturgy in the Western church is less representational, more symbolic, and it is as symbol that the maundy—the footwashing—has its deepest meaning.

We know that some early Christians included a footwashing in their baptismal rite. Use of the footwashing on the Thursday of the Triduum goes back to at least 697, when in Spain and Gaul the bishops and clergy were required to imitate their monastic brothers by washing the feet of their poor or of their community. As the centuries went on, only the higher clergy kept up the custom. Eventually only a few highly placed men washed the feet of 12 carefully selected men, and that was that. The ritual had so lost its intent that news reporters were astounded when John XXIII went into the slums of Rome to wash the dirty feet of some anonymous poor.

Perhaps because the rite came to be owned by the higher clergy, perhaps because passion plays easily supplant liturgy, some people who have revived the ceremony in our time teach that a single male should wash the feet of 12 people, perhaps the parish council. But at its most profound, the liturgy is neither clerical action nor representational drama. The church has understood that the maundy, the command, is not to wash one another's feet, but to love one another. We are not Christ and the disciples back at the Last Supper; we are the church in the present, and the footwashing can symbolize the loving community which in Christ we come to be.

There are various ways to enact the ceremony to make clear its communal intent. Some parishes use a number of stations, the persons getting their feet washed and then in turn washing the feet of the next. Even small children can participate, receiving help from an adult for the first several years. We might learn something from the Seventh Day Adventists, who hold a footwashing quarterly, with every service of holy communion, and who thus have developed the ceremony with gracious flow, involving all the baptized, with no sign of self-consciousness. However the footwashing is conducted, hymn singing heightens its communal nature and engages those worshipers who are not taking active part in the ceremony.

A hymn appropriate for the liturgy is "Ubi caritas," written during the ninth century to be sung during the maundy. Most hymnals include some version of the classic antiphon and its verses. The arrangement by Richard Proulx is excellent; the refrain, in Latin or English, allows for participation by those people processing or standing, washing or being washed. The Johannine refrain—that where is love, there is God—accentuates the symbolic interpretation of the maundy as God's love active in the community. The stanzas articulate the assembly's bond together in the love of Christ. Proulx utilized the chant long associated with this antiphon, while other versions are set to metered hymn tunes.

Another option for song during the maundy, or elsewhere in the service, is the newly-popular "Jesu, Jesu, fill us with your love." In the 1960s Tom Colvin, a Scottish Presbyterian missionary in Ghana, adapted a folk song of the Ghanaian people into this Maundy Thursday hymn. Colvin describes the birth of this song in this way:

> It came into being one night at Chereponi during a lay training course for a dozen or so evangelists, including two women, quite recently baptized themselves. . . . They brought forward this melody and thought it would well suit a song about God's love for all of us. Sitting there in the moonlight, I felt it simply had to be about black and white, rich and poor.

Colvin says that the songs were written for new Christians of all ages, "and I suppose we should all be that always."

With its refrain making participation possible by people who are liturgically busy, the hymn first evokes the scene of the Last Supper, as Jesus "kneels at the feet of his friends," then moves to the liturgical situation: "Loving puts us on our knees." The syntax is extremely simple without rendering the hymn puerile, and the words are bonded to the tune. As Colvin says of the words, "They cannot stand alone as words: They are songs, not poems set to music." For those Christians who wish during the maundy to make explicit Christ's modeling of community love, this hymn is ideal.

Furthermore, the African origin of "Jesu, Jesu" commends its use on this day. Colvin writes that his hymn tunes evolved from the boat songs which the men chant as they paddle their boats on the African rivers. It is appropriate that during the footwashing, adopting the stance of the ancient servant, the "haves" of the northern hemisphere join in the tune and the rhythm of the southerners they have repeatedly enslaved. Explaining the musical genre, Colvin writes that the "hymns should be sung as in Africa, shared between a leader or small group and the body of worshipers, the melody being exchanged between them." The verses overlap, the last note held as a drone by some singers while others sing the next verse. "In tunes so repetitive, it is usual for harmonies to be improvised spontaneously. . . . No melodic accompaniment is required: drums, percussion instruments, and sometimes clapping are all that are needed to support the voices." The song must not become a lament, dragging along, like "Michael, row the boat ashore" did.

"Ubi caritas" echoes down over the centuries, "Jesu, Jesu" calls to us from across the rivers and oceans. Both of these songs, with their verses and refrain, allow for participation by people liturgically busy. Both of these songs linger in the memory: Even after the ceremony of the maundy is completed by the community, the hymn will be repeating for hours in the minds of the people.

Sing, My Tongue

Sing, my tongue, the song of triumph,
  tell the story far and wide;
tell of dread and final battle,
sing of Savior crucified;
how upon the cross a victim
vanquishing in death he died.

He endured the nails, the spitting,
vinegar and spear and reed;
from that holy body broken
blood and water forth proceed:
earth and stars and sky and ocean
by that flood from stain are freed.

Faithful Cross, above all other,
one and only noble tree,
none in foliage, none in blossom,
none in fruit your peer may be;
sweet the wood and sweet the iron
and your load, most sweet is he.

Bend your boughs, O Tree of glory!
all your rigid branches, bend!
For a while the ancient temper
that your birth bestowed, suspend;
and the King of earth and heaven
gently on your bosom tend.

Venantius Fortunatus, tr. composite

There in God's Garden

There in God's garden stands the tree of wisdom
   whose leaves hold forth the healing of the nations:
tree of all knowledge, tree of all compassion,
   tree of all beauty.

Its name is Jesus, name that says "Our Savior":
there on its branches see the scars of suffering;
see where the tendrils of our human selfhood
   feed on its life-blood.

Thorns not its own are tangled in its foliage;
our greed has starved it, our despite has choked it.
Yet look, it lives! Its grief has not destroyed it,
   nor fire consumed it.

See how its branches reach to us in welcome;
hear what the voice says, "Come to me, ye weary!
Give me your sickness, give me all your sorrow.
   I will give blessing."

This is my ending; this my resurrection;
into your hands, Lord, I commit my spirit.
This have I searched for; now I can possess it.
 This ground is holy!

All heaven is singing, "Thanks to Christ whose passion
offers in mercy healing, strength and pardon:
peoples and nations, take it, take it freely!"
 Amen, my Master.

Kiràly Imre von Pécselyi, tr. Erik Routley

It seems that human religion has always known of the archetypal tree of life. Many cosmogonies tell of the primordial tree which grounds the universe. Ancient peoples described themselves as a tree of life, exalted enough to shelter all the birds of the air. Contemporary Bible translations make clear that the sacred pole, which periodically found its way into ancient Israelite worship, symbolized the Canaanite tree-of-life goddess Asherah. Egyptians painted on papyri a tree of life in which are perched five birds, one for each of the stages of human life; northern European peasant women danced around a tree-of-life pole to celebrate the fertility of spring; the Gbaya people of Cameroon ritualize reconciliation by giving one another a sprig from the soré tree, their tree of life; Black Elk foresaw that the Sioux tree of life was dying. How many legendary heroes and heroines must, for good or ill, pluck fruit from the tree of life? How many religious visionaries identify their inspiration with a tree?

The tree of life is alive and well. Carl Jung would not be surprised that an image could well up simultaneously in the consciousness of countless people, a metaphor of life arising from hibernation in a spiritually moribund society. For recently I see Hannah Cahoon's Shaker tree of life on book jackets and store signs and health food packaging; I read of Starhawk and other followers of the Craft conducting a tree-of-life ritual; the local gift shop sells classy wrapping paper on which a tree of life is superimposed on a globe, the map and the leaves intertwined, encircled by tigers and stars, bordered by branches. And rather than a dull typed list of the church's festivals, perhaps also you have on your wall a cosmic liturgical sphere, the seasons and festivals encircling a centered tree of life.

Marked on that liturgical circle is Good Friday, the premier paradox of the year. It is odd that we call the day of Christ's death good. The faithful assemble, not as usual in the morning or at a vigil, but midday, to conduct rituals unique to the day. Some Christians hold Good Friday as an absolute fast and refrain from communion; others commune with presanctified food, for on this day there is to be no great thanksgiving. As we commemorate the day on which Jesus was executed, we reproach ourselves for doing the killing. Yet on this day of death the church reads John's passion, in which Christ is a victorious king, crowned, robed, before whom the Roman soldiers fall down when he says, "Here I AM."

When visiting Jerusalem during the fourth century, the pilgrim Egeria participated in the veneration of the cross, which Queen Helena is said to have excavated from Calvary's hillside some decades before. Legend has it that the cross was hewn from a tree that grew from a seed that, at an angel's command, Adam's son took from Eden's tree of life. Like the palm procession Egeria experienced, the veneration of this life-giving tree was exported throughout Christendom, and in our churches we see Christians venerating not only relics of the true cross but bejeweled processional crosses of gold, or perhaps a life-sized wooden cross assembled last week by the youth group. It is a paradoxical day.

The early church did not have a cross-centered piety. The oldest depiction of a cross yet to be found is carved on the fourth-century door of St. Sabina church in Rome. That cross is objective, stylized: Christ stands peacefully, cross-shaped, arms outstretched. But as the centuries plodded on, and Christian guilt grew, a deathly crucifix became increasingly the dominant image in the churches, until late medieval crucifixions are all blood and gore, agony and suffering. The paradox of the good day was lost in a reverie of misery.

Fortunately in the treasury of Christian hymns are several gems to brighten our dour day, poems in which the cross is red not with the blood of death but with the fruit of life. For the greatest such hymn we go back to the sixth century, when the Germanic princess Radegund was kidnapped by the Christian Frankish king Chlotar and reared in a French convent to become one of his five queens. Despite Chlotar's barbarian manners and ethics, Radegund became highly educated, lived devoutly and finally separated from her husband to found a convent in Poitiers. She befriended a convert, Venantius Fortunatus, who as a young man had studied Latin rhetoric, oratory and poetry in Ravenna. He came to live in her abbey, and he wrote for the Queen both simple poems and magnificent hymns. When Radegund acquired for the abbey a relic of the true cross, he wrote "Vexilla Regis," "The royal banners forward go," and for the office during Holy Week he composed "Pange, lingua, gloriosi," "Sing, my tongue." In both hymns the poet Fortunatus reveres the cross as the archetypal tree of life.

Originally ten stanzas long, "Sing, my tongue" captures the paradox of Good Friday. Fortunatus begins with the image of Christ's death as a battle both lost and won, Christ as a victorious victim. Subsequent stanzas relate Christ's birth, life and death. One stanza seldom translated echoes the Passion Sunday proper preface, in which the attractive but forbidden tree in Eden is contrasted with the cross, the tree of life. In another stanza, the swaddling cloths are signs of the coming grave clothes. The blood and water do not drip piteously from Jesus' side; rather, through their flood the entire universe, "earth and stars and sky and ocean," are set free. Today we are not grieving but are singing triumphantly.

Most hymnals translate both tree-of-life stanzas. In the stanza "Faithful cross," the cross is viewed as more bounteously fruitful than any other tree of life. In the stanza "Bend your boughs," the tree becomes a loving motherly earth cradling the king on her bosom. The poem's success does not depend upon the assembly's emotional state; a metaphor proposes truth deeper than emotion. The metaphor of the tree of life allows for a vigorous poem of praise on the day of Jesus' death. By the way, Fortunatus wrote for Radegund an entire collection, *Hymns for All the Festivals of the Christian Year,* which has been lost, and a mighty loss it is.

Fortunatus was not the only hymnwriter whose cross was a tree of life. The seventeenth-century Hungarian Kiràly Imre von Pécselyi wrote "There in God's garden," which the modern hymnologist Erik Routley translated into English. The cross is the tree in God's garden, its leaves, as the Book of Revelation says, for the healing of the nations. As the stanzas progress it is not the cross, but Christ himself who is the tree, Christ who calls a blessing to us from its branches. The fifth stanza is a remarkable collage of sacred speech:

> This is my ending; this my resurrection;
> into your hands, Lord, I commit my spirit.
> This have I searched for; now I can possess it.
> This ground is holy.

Jesus' prayer at the moment of death is juxtaposed with God's call to Moses from another tree of life, the burning bush—"This ground is holy!" The words stutter out the paradox of the cross. Several tunes for this 11, 11, 11, 5 hymn are possible: Iste Confessor and Herzliebster Jesu are particularly appropriate.

For those Christians who observe Good Friday without any music, these hymns can find their place earlier in Holy Week or on September 14, the feast of the cross. But other Christians choose to observe Christ' death day by singing a cappella one of the hymns evoking the tree of life. In the spirit of John's gospel, the deadly cross bears fruit for the life of the whole world. These hymns are a good way to mark the paradox.

Come, Ye Faithful

Come, ye faithful, raise the strain of triumphant gladness;
God hath brought forth Israel into joy from sadness;
loosed from Pharaoh's bitter yoke Jacob's sons and daughters;
led them with unmoistened foot through the Red Sea waters.

'Tis the spring of souls today; Christ hath burst his prison,
and from three days' sleep in death as a sun hath risen;
all the winter of our sins, long and dark, is flying
from his light, to whom we give laud and praise undying.

Now the queen of seasons, bright with the day of splendor,
with the royal feast of feasts, comes its joy to render;
comes to glad Jerusalem, who with true affection
welcomes in unwearied strains Jesus' resurrection.

Neither might the gates of death, nor the tomb's dark portal,
nor the watchers, nor the seal hold thee as mortal;
but today amidst the twelve thou didst stand, bestowing
that thy peace which evermore passeth human knowing.

"Alleluia!" now we cry to our King immortal,
who, triumphant, burst the bars of the tomb's dark portal;
"Alleluia!" with the Son, God the Father praising,
"Alleluia!" yet again to the Spirit raising.

John of Damascus, tr. John Mason Neale

O Mary, Don't You Weep

O Mary, don't you weep, don't you mourn;
O Mary, don't you weep, don't you mourn;
Pharaoh's army got drownded,
O Mary, don't you weep.

One of these mornings bright and fair,
goin'-a take my wings and cleave the air;
Pharaoh's army got drownded,
O Mary, don't you weep.

When I get to heaven goin'-a sing and shout,
ain't nobody there goin'-a turn me out;
Pharaoh's army got drownded,
O Mary, don't you weep.

When I get to heaven goin'-a put on my shoes,
goin'-a run about and spread the news;
Pharaoh's army got drownded,
O Mary, don't you weep.

anon.

With the restoration of the paschal vigil, our Easter focus has radically shifted. As a child I wore a daffodil corsage to the 11 AM service, holding my breath for the aspiring trumpeter during the Hallelujah chorus and hearing a sermon that traced the movements of the Marys and the men on the first Easter morning. Harmonizing the gospel accounts was part of following in the steps of Jesus. I recall being delighted by the quite different homily of my first Easter vigil: I was not accustomed to such metaphoric and sacramental brilliance! I discovered later that with uncharacteristic humility the preacher, rather than composing his own sermon, had read us the homily of John Chrysostom. "The calf is fatted: let no one go away hungry," sounded an Easter in a key both higher and deeper than that of our choir's attempt at Handel.

Like the footwashing, the vigil demonstrates that liturgy is not about dramatic representation of events in the life of Jesus. It is not about tracing the steps of the Marys but rather about being the church. Thus to enact most fully what it means to live in the resurrection, we assemble in the world's darkness, hear the narratives of redemption, baptize and commune together. Of course, we read the story of the empty tomb, or the vision of angels, or the appearances of Jesus. But our minds find the meaning of these accounts difficult to grasp.

Thus the vigil relies on metaphors to carry the celebration. Metaphor, said the American poet Wallace Stevens, is the tension produced when talking about two different things at the same time. Metaphor is saying something startlingly true about A by talking instead about B. By using inappropriate words, our speech becomes profoundly truthful. How to say that we live surrounded by death? We gather at night. How to praise the brilliance of the resurrection? We honor a candle. We live out the metaphor, and we fill our ritual with metaphoric speech.

The primary metaphor for Christ's resurrection is the passover. The story says that an ancient people were enslaved; God summoned a family of three to bring off salvation; with Moses striding and Miriam singing and Aaron praying, the people crossed the tumultuous sea of chaos and death to dance on the safe side of the sea. We all know the story; its overtones and harmonies resonate throughout religious history from one imagination to another. God saved Israel, God saved Jesus, God saved us, and God is saving the catechumens standing here before us. We need not go back to a previous holy time: The time of God's salvation is today, is every time. On our candle is this year's date, our moment for the Alpha and the Omega. The ancient story, told over and over, gives the present tongue-tied reality its words. The ancient story is metaphor for our experience.

In the eighth century there lived in Jerusalem a Greek monk and theologian, famous as one of the greatest Christian hymnwriters of all time. Hymns for the office developed differently in the East than in the West. In the East the hymns, known as canons, were mammothly long odes—Eastern worship cares not about the clock— characterized by elaborate meters and interwoven biblical imagery. John of Damascus composed such an ode for the second Sunday of Easter, and from its many lines John Mason Neale shaped the Easter hymn "Come, ye faithful, raise the strain." With enough facets to reflect the many brilliancies of the festival, the hymn accomplishes its task with metaphor.

The first stanza employs passover imagery. Easter is the passover made available to Christians. This is the night, we sing at the vigil, joining with devout Jews at their seder praising God for tonight's redemption. Christian use of Jewish imagery need not foster anti-Semitic reflection. Rather, we Christians honor the experience of our Jewish cousins when we borrow their stories as metaphors for our experience of divine grace. Several hymnal committees have edited out some of John of Damascus's biblical references, I suppose afraid that our people cannot think metaphorically. Neale's version says that Christ comes today to "glad Jerusalem" and that he stands "amidst the twelve." Well, yes, there are not twelve on Easter, back then or now. Rather, "the twelve" is a way to refer to all the faithful, then and now. "Jerusalem" signifies not the conflicted twentieth-century city, but this assembly, and every assembly, receiving the resurrected Christ. Can our people learn to love these metaphors?

John of Damascus uses not only biblical metaphors. Our sins are winter, the resurrection is spring. Our life was dark, Christ is the rising sun. Death is an evil prison, Christ the triumphant liberator. The last stanza employs the same imagery as the Orthodox icon of the resurrection. Christ "bursts the bars of the tomb's dark portal"—the icons picture Christ standing astride the broken doors of the pit of death.

No contemporary Christians embrace this metaphoric use of Hebrew imagery more fully than African Americans. During their centuries as slaves of Christian overlords, they found in the narratives of the Hebrew people the metaphors for their life and faith. Spirituals like "There is a balm in Gilead" and "Swing low, sweet chariot" exemplify this borrowing of Jewish imagery for Christian purposes. Still today the black preachers' use of the Hebrew scriptures displays an interest not in scholarly accuracy or allegorical illustration, but in metaphoric appropriation. If you never hear this tradition of preaching, you can read it in James Baldwin's *Go Tell It on the Mountain.*

Although the black Protestant churches have not revived the vigil, the African American spiritual "O Mary, don't you weep" captures the vigil's metaphors with a style profound and simple. "O Mary, don't you weep, don't you mourn" begins the hymn, and we imagine Mary of Magdala encountering the strange gardener. "Pharaoh's army got drownded," and we recall Miriam's dance after the escape from slavery. "When I get to heaven goin'-a sing and shout," and we stand with the newly baptized rejoicing in salvation, for this is the night when all the people are saved. The ancient story, the gospel narrative, our assembly and our hope for salvation are held together by the metaphors in the spiritual.

The music of black spirituals is itself a metaphor. American slaves were encouraged by their white masters to sing as they worked, and for such song the slaves relied on the African rhythms of their past freedom to express their communal suffering and Christian hope. The relatively easy melody line and meter of spirituals serves as communal support for individual ornamentation and syncopation. Individual freedom enriches communal participation. Repetition grounds improvisation. For those Christians who can sing it well, this genre symbolizes the song of the assembly.

In a world which knows such endless death, such deep misery, such wide suffering, we need more than potted lilies, Easter egg hunts and the Hallelujah chorus to proclaim the resurrection. Such unequivocal signs of life will not suffice. We need, rather, the ambivalence of metaphors that begin in death, that know misery, and yet tell of divine salvation. Tulips are too young to know of death. But the passover imagery of the sufferings of the Israelites and the Egyptians: Here is a metaphor to contain our life for another year.

This Day God Gives Me

This day God gives me
strength of high heaven,
sun and moon shining,
flame in my hearth,
flashing of lightning,
wind in its swiftness,
deeps of the ocean,
firmness of earth.

This day God sends me
strength as my guardian,
might to uphold me,
wisdom as guide.
Your eyes are watchful,
your ears are list'ning,
your lips are speaking,
friend at my side.

God's way is my way,
God's shield is round me,
God's host defends me,
saving from ill.

Angels of heaven,
drive from me always
all that would harm me,
stand by me still.

Rising, I thank you,
mighty and strong One,
King of creation,
Giver of rest,
firmly confessing
Threeness of Persons,
Oneness of Godhead,
Trinity blest.

asc. Patrick, tr. James Quinn

Amazing Grace

Amazing grace! How sweet the sound
that saved a wretch like me!
I once was lost, but now am found;
was blind, but now I see.

'Twas grace that taught my heart to fear,
and grace my fears relieved;
how precious did that grace appear
the hour I first believed.

Through many dangers, toils, and snares,
I have already come;
'tis grace hath brought me safe thus far,
and grace will lead me home.

The Lord has promised good to me,
his word my hope secures;
he will my shield and portion be,
as long as life endures.

Yea, when this flesh and heart shall fail,
and mortal life shall cease,
I shall possess, within the veil,
a life of joy and peace.

When we've been there ten thousand years,
bright shining as the sun,
we've no less days to sing God's praise
than when we'd first begun.

John Newton, stanza 6 anon.

It is not that catechumens can be baptized only at the paschal vigil. Rather, it is that at the vigil the meaning of baptism is most fully celebrated. Baptism illumines those who wait in this world's darkness, births from God's womb those who will live anew, drowns what is moribund in the self and forms human fragments into a divine body. The liturgy of songs and readings in the night of the resurrection contains these meanings, and so, reviving the practice of the early Christians, we baptize at the vigil.

We baptize both infants and adults, thereby affirming two paradigms of how humans experience God's grace. Some of the baptized are newborns brought into the church by believing parents for whom nurturance in the church is part of family life. These babies are born again from a second womb, and in their helplessness before the terrors of the world recall for us the might of God's mercy before and beyond our knowing. Baptism places the infants in the divine embrace and hands them to the church for nursing.

On the other hand, some catechumens are adults who walk or run or stagger into the church after years of struggle and months of instruction. These adults drown their old life and wash its rot away, and by their acceptance of the church's communal life remind us that when the Spirit breathes into the boneyard, new beings arise to praise. Through baptism these believers embrace God and join with all the assembly to share the feast.

A classic hymn text appropriate for the baptism of an infant is St. Patrick's Breastplate. Christian tradition says that Patrick, born in the fourth century of a noble Roman family, forced into slavery for six years, became the first missionary to Ireland. We do not know many details of the ancient Celtic religion—a three-personed fertility goddess was revered, the druids were a priestly class with considerable religious and political knowledge. Legend, however, has it that one Easter Eve, as Patrick was striking the paschal light, he was surrounded by druids; he uttered his famous prayer for protection; and God saved him from capture. We sing his Breast-plate on Easter Eve to this day.

Several quite different translations of this ancient Christian entreaty are available. Cecil Frances Alexander, known for her children's songs like "There is a green hill far away," is responsible for the long version, "I bind unto myself today." The singers bond themselves to the power of God's name, the power of Christ's life and death, the power of the angels and saints, the power of the created order. In the fifth stanza, an anthropomorphized God holds and leads, watches and hears, teaches and guides, gives safety and speech. The last stanza is yet another incantation in which Christ is the all-embracing and all-powerful protection. The words are rugged: they sound over the centuries like Celtic charms, invoking divine power in the face of myriad forces of evil. The tone is primitive, a spell to carve over a child's cradle, a formula for the soldier as he dons his breastplate. The tune tied to Alexander's translation is an adapted Irish air.

A much shorter and livelier version, set to the popular lilting Gaelic melody Bunessan, captures the primordial sound of entreaty. Each short phrase calls on yet another divine gift:

This day God sends me
strength as my guardian,
might to uphold me,
wisdom as guide.

In the longer version, as Patrick responds to the Celtic deities, we affirm the mystery of the divine name as the power of Threeness and Oneness. St. Patrick's Breast-plate thus provides us with an ancient Trinitarian baptismal hymn with language other than "Father, Son, and Spirit," and Quinn's translation, by being cast in second person address to God, eliminates the 11 uses of "his" in the nineteenth-century version.

A very different hymn portrays an image of the adult convert. "Amazing grace" has become a phenomenally popular song for white and black Christians alike. The hymn was composed in 1779 by John Newton, at that time an Anglican cleric in Olney, England, who collaborated with William Cowper to write hundreds of evangelical hymns. Newton, who had lived like a seaman in a Robert Louis Stevenson adventure tale, was a slave trader for six years before responding to the preaching of the Wesleys. Newton wrote extensive journals and letters, describing the "wretch" he had been before being stunned into a life shaped by God's mercy. The hymn's affectively simple English prose speaks of his adult conversion and his subsequent reliance on grace.

Many people attest to the inexplicable incantatory power of "Amazing grace." Johnny Cash, singing it for prison inmates, describes it as a talisman; he says: "These are words without guile." The purity of the pentatonic melody allows for the hymn to be sung either in childlike simplicity or with improvised ornamentation and various harmonic styles. Because the tune is so familiar, singers can provide only ornamentation, for the melody holds its own within our imagination. Writers after Newton added to his stanzas: some hymnals include a final stanza that anticipates the joys of heaven and makes explicit the community of believers. The hymn exemplifies the church's use, reuse and adaptation of an individual's composition and is thus a good symbol for the life of the baptized.

We sing at the vigil as if we were Miriam dancing at the sea. Here are two other songs, one as if we were a mother in ancient times, begging for the beneficent powers to protect herself and her newborn, and one as if we were a reformed slave trader, bearing a past of untold misery and sin. Of course, each image is true: We are a mother praying for protection as well as a slave trader pleading for mercy. As the newly baptized process around the assembly, we sing these hymns to bond us to this truth, to our baptismal promises, to Patrick and John Newton, and to one another.

O Holy Spirit, by Whose Breath

Holy Spirit, by whose breath
life rises vibrant out of death;
come to create, renew, inspire;
come, kindle in our hearts your fire.

You are the seeker's sure resource,
of burning love the living source,
protector in the midst of strife,
the giver and the Lord of life.

In you God's energy is shown,
to us your varied gifts made known.
Teach us to speak, teach us to hear;
yours is the tongue and yours the ear.

Flood our dull senses with your light;
in mutual love our hearts unite.
Your power the whole creation fills;
confirm our weak, uncertain wills.

From inner strife grant us release;
turn nations to the ways of peace.
To fuller life your people bring
that as one body we may sing:

Praise to the Father, Christ, his Word,
and to the Spirit: God the Lord,
to whom all honor, glory be
both now and for eternity.

Rabanus Maurus, tr. John Grant

Come Down, O Love Divine

Come down, O Love divine,
seek thou this soul of mine,
and visit it with thine own ardor glowing;
O Comforter, draw near,
within my heart appear,
and kindle it, thy holy flame bestowing.

O let it freely burn,
till earthly passions turn
to dust and ashes in its heat consuming;
and let thy glorious light
shine ever on my sight,
and clothe me round, the while my path illuming.

And so the yearning strong,
with which the soul will long,
shall far outpass the power of human telling;
for none can guess its grace,
till Love create a place
wherein the Holy Spirit makes a dwelling.

Bianco da Siena, tr. Richard Littledale

Pentecost, the conclusion to the 50 days of Easter, offers yet another way to proclaim the resurrection: The Spirit of Christ, far from being dead and buried, is alive and well in the body of Christ. We see that body and experience that Spirit in the Christian community, as well as in its symbol of shared bread and wine. The focus of the day is on invocation: If on Easter Day we acclaim the empty tomb and laud the risen one, on Pentecost we beseech the Spirit to live not only in Galilee but also within this assembly.

Pentecost became identified with church-building events such as confirmation and ordination. The idea of God alive in the church made the day red with the flames of the Spirit. The liturgical texts are filled with the rush of wind and the Spirit's breath. But felt doves on burlap banners hardly send us flying into divine realms. Pentecost is one festival for which our hymnody does far better than our other arts to convey the intent of the day. We have a rich treasury of hymns that brilliantly invokes the endless life of the risen Spirit.

The mother of these invocations is the ninth-century "Veni Creator Spiritus." Historical consensus credits this hymn to Rabanus Maurus, a German Benedictine teacher and abbot, who wrote not only hymns, but a glossary of the Bible, commentaries on the Old and New Testaments and a life of Mary of Magdala. "Veni Creator Spiritus" has been appointed for use during the week of Pentecost since the tenth century and at special ceremonies since the eleventh. Dozens of translations exist. Our current hymnals publish versions under the following titles: "O Holy Spirit by whose breath," "Creator Spirit, by whose aid," "Creator Spirit, heavenly dove," "Come, Holy Ghost, our souls inspire," "Come, Holy Ghost, Creator blest," and "Come, Creator Spirit, highly blest." With the variety of translations available, one must check the index for Rabanus Maurus or "Veni Creator Spiritus" in order to locate the hymn.

Deism, a heresy popular among the American founding fathers, suggested that God created the world eons ago but has been in retirement since recorded history. On Pentecost, we affirm the opposite, that God keeps on creating. We invoke the sevenfold gifts of the Spirit; we beseech the Spirit to pour upon us light, love and power. We stand in the place of Jesus, receiving God's anointing for our life as the royal family in the dominion of God. We pray for the whole world: "from inner strife, grant us release; turn nations to the ways of peace." On this day we pray that everyone come "to fuller life."

From the thirteenth century comes the preeminently ecclesiastical Golden Sequence, composed for the liturgy and used especially at ordinations. "Veni Sancte Spiritus," an elaboration on the Alleluia verse, invokes the Spirit who is light, consolation, refreshment, repose. Everything in need is held up for the Spirit's gift of life: The Spirit will cool what is hot, cleanse what is soiled, water what is dry, heal what is wounded, "melt the frozen, warm the chill," says Peter Scagnelli's translation. One tradition urges singers to kneel while singing this invocation.

Remember the Christmas carols of the fourteenth century? The emerging lay spirit of that time produced not only ring dancers, but the intriguing Flagellants. These groups of lay Christians, sometimes organized into lay orders, caused the hierarchy considerable distress, because their socially powerful activities occurred beyond and outside clerical control. The disasters of the fourteenth century, notably the Black Plague, were popularly interpreted as divine punishments, and the Flagellants processed around the cities and countryside, whipping themselves and appealing for divine aid. They had imbibed what we would consider excessive guilt, even self-hatred; yet they took to the streets with a newly claimed power and growing lay awareness. As they marched, they sang vernacular hymns to simple tunes, often referred to as Laudi hymns. The most famous of these is an invocation of the Spirit, "Come down, O Love divine."

We hear this hymn in Siena, where the plague killed 40 percent of the population and the cathedral was left uncompleted to this day. This is the Siena of Catherine, herself traversing the countryside on her own authority, singing to the Trinity as her table, her food and her waiter. Written about 1400 by a Flagellant named Bianco da Siena, "Come down, O Love divine" invokes God's Spirit as a kindling love that will burn away what is dross to leave a bright and purified self in which God resides. The picture of God's visiting the community of the faithful, found in the classic "Veni Creator Spiritus" and "Veni Sancte Spiritus," gives way to the image of the individual's faithful heart burning with adoration. Contemporary Christians sing the hymn to a lush and lovely tune composed in 1906 by the great English church musician Ralph Vaughn Williams and named for his childhood village, Down Ampney.

Hymnwriters continue to compose creative invocations. We have Tom Colvin's African "Spirit-friend," James Manley's "Spirit of gentleness, Spirit of restlessness," Aelred Seton's "Love of our Abba," Miriam Therese Winter's "Wellspring of wisdom, Dawn of a new day, and Garden of grace," and the Dakota hymn to the "star-abiding One." But inspiring these hymnwriters to sing, enflaming our invocation of the Spirit on the church and our hearts, is still an old Benedictine abbot teaching the Bible and the unruly Flagellants beating themselves for God.

THE YEAR

Ordinary Time

... Leaning
on the
everlasting
arms ...

"What a fellowship,"
Elisha Hoffman

Ye Watchers and Ye Holy Ones

Ye watchers and ye holy ones,
    bright seraphs, cherubim, and thrones,
raise the glad strain, Alleluia!
Cry out, dominions, princedoms, powers,
virtues, archangels, angels' choirs,
    Alleluia, alleluia, alleluia, alleluia, alleluia.

O higher than the cherubim,
more glorious than the seraphim,
lead their praises, Alleluia!
Thou bearer of the eternal Word,
most gracious, magnify the Lord,
    Alleluia, alleluia, alleluia, alleluia, alleluia.

Respond, ye souls in endless rest,
ye patriarchs and prophets blest,
Alleluia, alleluia!
Ye holy twelve, ye martyrs strong,
all saints triumphant, raise the song,
    Alleluia, alleluia, alleluia, alleluia, alleluia.

O friends, in gladness let us sing,
supernal anthems echoing,
Alleluia, alleluia!
To God the Father, God the Son,
and God the Spirit, Three in One:
 Alleluia, alleluia, alleluia, alleluia, alleluia.

J. Athelstan Riley

Mary the Dawn

Mary the dawn, Christ the perfect day;
Mary the gate, Christ the heavenly way!

Mary the root, Christ the mystic vine;
Mary the grape, Christ the sacred wine!

Mary the wheat, Christ the living bread;
Mary the stem, Christ the rose blood-red!

Mary the font, Christ the cleansing flood;
Mary the cup, Christ the saving blood!

Mary the temple, Christ the temple's lord;
Mary the shrine, Christ the God adored!

Mary the beacon, Christ the haven's rest;
Mary the mirror, Christ the vision blest!

Mary the mother, Christ the mother's Son,
By all things blest while endless ages run.

Paul Cross

On the campus green at a Roman Catholic university in Philadelphia are two statues of Mary. One depicts the appearance of Mary to Bernadette at Lourdes. Mary is pure white, veiled, praying, holding a rosary, framed by a stone grotto, adored by a second statue of a kneeling child. The shrine calls us to pray, along with the child, to our Mother in humility. The other statue is a rough-finished bronze casting of a larger-than-life old woman striding across the lawn. This "Walking Madonna" by the British sculptor Elizabeth Frink stops us in our tracks: She has lived longer and stronger than we have, and the statue beckons us to try to catch up. Those Christians who sing hymns about or to Mary can choose from dozens of hymns that exemplify the first statue. But such hymns, although beloved by some communities, are troublesome in two ways.

One problem occurs when Mary is depicted as solely divine. It is easy to understand how during the Middle Ages, with power in the church overwhelmingly male and with the God of popular piety a terrifying king, Mary became a goddess figure. Contemplating the cathedrals of Notre Dame in Paris and Chartres, we are astounded by the centrality of devotion to this goddess. But we also know from studying goddess religions that male worship of the feminine divine, far from accruing any benefit to the women in the culture, often left the women groveling in the dust. We cannot continue the Mary-goddess tradition unconsciously any longer. As a nun said to me, "Salve Regina: but 'Regina'—that's God." When God is no longer a stern heavenly king, we need no moderating heavenly queen. When God is no longer solely the archetypal father, we need no parallel archetypal mother.

A second problem inherent in much Marian hymnody is the celibate bias. Already in hymnwriters like Ambrose, Mary is revered for sexual abstinence. Again, the development of "the Virgin undefiled" language is understandable, in light of the church's ideal of asceticism and the increasingly celibate clergy. But modern biblical scholarship has demonstrated that Matthew's and Luke's language of the virgin birth is about Christ's identity, not about rejection of sexual intercourse. It was about the eleventh century that Mary's "purity" meant no longer her goodness but her sexual abstinence, and we can no longer repeat this interpretation unconsciously. One must wonder what singing such hymns which laud sexual abstinence has done to the consciousness of the faithful laywomen who were given as their life's work the bearing of children.

While most of the ways Mary has been honored in the Christian tradition occur outside or beyond the eucharistic liturgy, there are several festivals associated with Mary for which some good hymnody must be sought. August 15, the date observed as Mary's death day, although variously titled, is now also on the calendar of some Protestant churches. In some traditions, Mary features prominently on February 2, popularly called Candlemas. The Visitation, May 31, and the fourth Sunday of Advent in years B and C offer other occasions to emulate Mary's praise of God. Fortunately there are several hymns which avoid the various pitfalls.

Perhaps the finest Christian hymn lauding Mary is "Ye watchers and ye holy ones." Written in 1906 by an Anglican layman named J. Athelstan Riley, "Ye watchers" makes available for us in the West Riley's deep attraction to Eastern Christian imagery of praise. The first stanza calls on all nine ranks of angels to praise God. The nine ranks derive from Jewish apocalyptic imagination and are named in different ways by the church fathers. Usually the ranks include the seraphim, who are burning fires around the divine throne; the cherubim, often depicted as winged bulls; thrones; dominions; princedoms; powers; virtues, who are the angels in charge of miracles on earth; archangels, sometimes named as Michael, Gabriel, Raphael and Uriel; and lastly, regular angels. Riley's first stanza begins by evoking the watchers, or holy ones, a name given about a century before the birth of Christ to those powerful angels who, never sleeping, watch over human affairs. Riley's third stanza calls on all the saints, the patriarchs, prophets, the twelve, and the martyrs, to praise, and the last stanza includes the present singing assembly.

For his second stanza Riley versified the Eastern church's Theotokion, the office hymn to Mary. The hymn says that Mary, part of the human creation, is acclaimed higher than the highest ranks of angels: Because of the incarnation, she is closer to God than even the heavenly beings. She is "bearer of the eternal Word." She is "most gracious," and she leads our praises with her Magnificat. I recall singing this stanza as a small child, loving the sound of the words, but quite ignorant that my ardent song was lauding Mary.

Riley composed his words for the seventeenth-century tune Lasst Uns Erfreuen, one of the most magnificent tunes in the Christian repertoire. The tune well illustrates that even the simplest scale patterns, if brilliantly arranged and rhythmically designed, can succeed for powerful congregational song.

In 1947, the Passionist Justin Mulcahy, using the pen name Paul Cross, wrote a quite different hymn. In his responsorial chant "Mary the dawn," the choir sings out its 13 images of Mary, and the congregation responds with 13 images of Christ. The choir recalls the Marian tradition, and the assembly responds with a deeper Christology. The poetic images are richly evocative. Natural images—dawn leads to day, wheat leads to bread—and Christian images—grapes lead to wine, font leads to flood—bring Marian devotion into eucharistic devotion. Mary is "the mother" without becoming "Our Mother." "Mary the dawn" is the Litany of Loretto brought to Christ, a striking Marian hymn for those whose piety calls for one.

If Mary were asked, she'd likely urge us simply to sing her Magnificat. Luke places this Hebrew praise of the saving God in the mouth of the exultant Mary. Monastic communities and those praying the breviary sing the Magnificat daily, but eucharistic assemblies—the vast majority of Christians—seldom do. All our hymnals offer at least one version of Mary's Magnificat. Inclusive language translations are found in some chant settings and in versifications by James Quinn, Timothy Dudley-Smith and Miriam Therese Winter. With these chants and hymns we join the walking Madonna, singing to God as she strides through the world. We honor Mary as the prototype of the lowly woman, the oppressed poor, whom God saves. But in singing her Magnificat we magnify not mainly her, but the God whom she magnifies.

For All the Saints

For all the saints, who from their labors rest,
  who thee by faith before the world confessed,
thy Name, O Jesus, be forever blessed.
    Alleluia, alleluia.

Thou wast their rock, their fortress, and their might:
thou, Lord, their Captain in the well-fought fight;
thou, in the darkness drear, the one true Light.
    Alleluia, alleluia.

O may thy soldiers, faithful, true, and bold,
fight as the saints who nobly fought of old,
and win, with them, the victor's crown of gold.
    Alleluia, alleluia.

O blest communion, fellowship divine!
We feebly struggle, they in glory shine;
Yet all are one in thee, for all are thine.
    Alleluia, alleluia.

And when the strife is fierce, the warfare long,
steals on the ear the distant triumph song,
and hearts are brave again, and arms are strong.
    Alleluia, alleluia.

The golden evening brightens in the west;
soon, soon to faithful warriors cometh rest;
sweet is the calm of paradise the blest.
    Alleluia, alleluia.

But lo! there breaks a yet more glorious day;
the saints triumphant rise in bright array;
the King of glory passes on his way.
    Alleluia, alleluia.

From earth's wide bounds, from ocean's farthest coast,
through gates of pearl streams in the countless host,
singing to Father, Son, and Holy Ghost.
    Alleluia, alleluia.

William W. How

Camina, Pueblo De Dios
Walk on, O people of God

Camina, pueblo de Dios,
camina, pueblo de Dios.
Nueva ley, nueva alianza,
en la nueva creación.
Camina, pueblo de Dios,
camina, pueblo de Dios.

Mira allá en el Calvario
en la roca hay una cruz;
muerte que engendra la vida,
nuevos hombres, nueva luz.
Cristo nos ha salvado
con su muerte y resurrección.
Todas las cosas renacen
en la nueva creación.

Cristo toma en su cuerpo
el pecado, la esclavitud.
Al destruirlos, nos trae
una nueva plenitud.
Pone en paz a los hombres,
a las cosas y al Creador.

Todo renace a la vida
en la nueva creación.

Cielo y tierra se abrazan,
nuestra alma halla el perdón.
Vuelven a abrirse los cielos
para el hombre pecador.
Israel peregrino,
vive y canta tu redención.
Hay nuevos mundos abiertos
en la nueva creación.

Walk on, O people of God;
walk on, O people of God.
A new law, God's new alliance,
all creation is reborn.
Walk on, O people of God;
walk on, O people of God.

Look on Calvary's summit;
on the rock there towers a cross;
death that gives birth to new living,
a new people, a new light.
Christ has brought us salvation
with his death and rising again.
Everything comes to new birthing,
all creation is reborn.

Christ takes into his body
all our sin, enslavement, and pain;
as he destroys them he brings us
life's abundance, life's new joy.
Christ brings reconciliation
to all things and people with God.
Nature bursts into new flowering,
all creation is reborn.

Heaven and earth are embracing,
and our souls find pardon at last.
Now heaven's gates are reopened
to the sinner, to us all,

Israel walks a journey;
now we live, salvation's our song;
Christ's resurrection has freed us.
There are new worlds to explore.

Cesareo Gabarain, tr. George Lockwood

One of the ways humankind celebrates itself is to march around. Scout troops and fife and drum corps march to the local park on the Fourth of July. Some of us recall John Kennedy on Inauguration Day striding down Constitution Avenue, rather than riding in the presidential limousine. Couples who have chosen the most casual life styles appeal for the Hesitation Step on their wedding day, as if a grand march will symbolize the archetypal grandeur their lives lack. A march proclaims, "This is who we are, we know where we are going, and we are having a grand time of it all." In a disillusioned and fragmented age, there are few parades; but when the church remembers its saints, there is at least the metaphor of a march to contain our celebration.

The nineteenth century saw the composition of many Christian marching songs. Sabine Baring-Gould crafted his "Onward Christian Soldiers" to accompany the marching of children from his village to the next for a Sunday school rally. When we hear "When the saints go marching in," we think of jazz musicians strutting down the street, but usually the marching hymns utilize military imagery. "The Battle Hymn of the Republic" and "Stand up, stand up for Jesus" are such marching songs, which imagine the faithful as a triumphant army conquering evil and manifesting truth. The genre continued into this century, with "Lift high the cross" linking baptism to enlistment into the victorious army.

To understand why many Christian marching songs incorporate military imagery, we must go back to one of the earliest saints to be venerated, Martin of Tours, famed as a soldier who quit the army to become a soldier for Christ. Martyrs were venerated for having died for the faith: By extension, those who nobly lived through their struggles came to be described as soldiers. Baptismal exorcisms depicted life as a battle against the powers of Satan. The imagery tends toward unequivocal exhilaration: The Christian army is all good, all victorious; evil is clearly recognized and eventually vanquished. Christians march in unmitigated pride: To sing these marches we are to be exuberant in song, united in spirit. There is no room in these texts or tunes for doubters. Here the victorious hymn, not the mysteriously complex assembly, is in charge.

Pastoral issues abound. The national news media has monitored the battles within our churches as committees debated whether to include these warlike hymns in new hymnals. Usually the committee voted no, and thousands of Christians marched toward headquarters shouting yes. How much do these hymns maintain in modern consciousness the ancient glorification of warfare? In Anglo-Saxon, the language spoken in the British Isles in the year 1000, the word for man was identical with the word for warrior. Presumably we have come along a bit since then. But we are still transfixed by films of D-Day, when soldiers, mostly dying, some surviving, ran up the beaches and scaled the cliffs straight into enemy fire, for we know there was indeed an enemy, and it had to be vanquished. Military imagery is not obsolete, but we must use it with care. "A soldier in God's army" must be recognized as a metaphor, a synonym for "a fruit on the tree of life" or "an infant nursing at God's breast," and not as divine sanction for military solutions to international woes. The metaphor must never be literalized, the Christians of one nation assuming that God's weapons are their own, to brandish in the world's political power plays.

These hymns also tend to praise not God but the church. While the focus is sometimes on the dead Christians who have already conquered, the circle usually includes the present congregation, marching with those who are already victorious. People love these hymns because it is fun to acclaim ourselves triumphant. For all these reasons, such marches must be selected and scheduled with care.

Perhaps the greatest of these hymns is "For all the saints," written in 1864 by William W. How, an Anglican bishop renowned for his ministry among the poor of his diocese. The hymn's military imagery is set in a wider context: Christ is rock, light and calm as well as fortress, captain, rest and king. The image of warfare is fully developed into a narrative: in stanza 2 the soldiers are in darkness; in stanza 4 we "feebly struggle"; in stanza 5 the "strife is fierce"; in stanza 6 the battle is over, and the warriors rest; in stanza 7 the conquering king arrives; and in the last stanza all the victors enter through the triumphal gates into the city. The text continually turns its attention to Christ, praising not the self or the church but God. "For all the saints," favored for All Saints' Day, was set by Ralph Vaughan Williams in 1906 to the simple but glorious tune Sine Nomine. Depending on the accompaniment, the stanzas can convey the lyrical feel of the "golden evening," as well as rouse us all up for the march into heaven.

The genre continues to this day. In 1987, Cesareo Gabarain, a Spanish musician and parish priest, wrote "Camina, pueblo de Dios." The hymn appears with an English translation in several new hymnals and is a worthy addition to any collection. There are two different situations in which primarily English-speaking congregations might sing non-English hymns. When Lutherans dust off a German they have not spoken for several generations to warble "Stille Nacht" at Christmastime, the danger is that nostalgia imprisons the incarnation in an ethnic past. But when a bilingual assembly sings—perhaps alternate stanzas, perhaps simultaneously in both languages—in Spanish and English, we are more genuinely marching together into a future world, one in which we are told Christianity will thrive in the southern hemisphere and English theologians will listen to the gospel preached by Hispanic missionaries.

"Camina, pueblo de Dios," "Walk on, O people of God," calls for the church to respond to God's new creation. The marching mood is alive and well; yet the hymn contains no military imagery. The hill of Calvary brings new birth, the resurrection gives reconcilation. It is interesting to contrast Gabarain's last stanza with How's last two. In How's hymn, the victorious soldiers are marching through the triumphal arch. In Gabarain's hymn, the Exsultet is recalled as heaven and earth embrace, and we march in through heaven's gates, not as into a rest after a battle but into a new world awaiting our exploration, for "all creation is reborn."

When the eucharistic assembly sings such marching songs, we are to acclaim not our nation, ethnic identity or opinion about military budgets but our God. The "arms" are weapons only if they are also God's embrace, an image of both military victory and blissful marriage. On saints' days, then, the march unites us to the faithful departed in both triumph and love.

All People That on Earth Do Dwell

All people that on earth do dwell,
sing to the Lord with cheerful voice.
Him serve with mirth, his praise forth tell;
come ye before him and rejoice.

Know that the Lord is God indeed;
without our aid he did us make;
we are his folk, he doth us feed,
and for his sheep he doth us take.

O enter then his gates with praise;
approach with joy his courts unto;
praise, laud, and bless his name always,
for it is seemly so to do.

For why! the Lord our God is good;
his mercy is forever sure;
his truth at all times firmly stood,
and shall from age to age endure.

William Kethe

O God, Our Help in Ages Past

O God, our help in ages past,
   our hope for years to come,
our shelter from the stormy blast,
and our eternal home:

Under the shadow of thy throne
thy saints have dwelt secure;
sufficient is thine arm alone,
and our defense is sure.

Before the hills in order stood,
or earth received her frame,
from everlasting thou art God,
to endless years the same.

A thousand ages in thy sight
are like an evening gone;
short as the watch that ends the night
before the rising sun.

Time, like an ever-rolling stream,
bears all our years away;
they fly, forgotten, as a dream
dies at the opening day.

O God, our help in ages past,
our hope for years to come,
be thou our guard while life shall last,
and our eternal home.

Isaac Watts

In 1634, John Lathrop, an English dissenting minister, having been released from prison on the proviso that he would leave England, arrived with his followers in the wilderness that is now Massachusetts. Like the famous Puritan pilgrims of 15 years before, Lathrop hoped to live out his own brand of Protestantism in peace, and he arrived on American shores singing psalms in gratitude for the chance to do so. Indeed, psalms were what he sang. Influenced by John Calvin, he believed that Christians ought to sing only metrical versions of the psalter in public worship. The psalms were surely the Word of God, no mere human invention. The psalms were filled with sacred metaphors—there are seven in the first two verses of Psalm 18 alone—images to express the mercy of God and the praise of the faithful. Wary lest any human additions slither back into worship, these dissenting Protestants stuck with the psalms, despite the ungainly, and at times wretched, translations they used.

Thus we read in Lathrop's journal a description of a day of Thanksgiving: "1 Decemb 22 1636 in ye Meetinghouse, beginning some half an houre before nine and continued untill after twelve a clocke, ye day beeing very cold, beginning with a short prayer, then a psalme sung, then more large in prayer, after that an other psalme, and then the word taught, after that prayer—& then a psalme." One can understand why metrical psalms were so essential in this Calvinist piety: The sung psalter provided the only breaks to the voice of the minister praying and preaching for hours on end.

Such late autumn celebrations of communal thanksgiving we know best through the myths of the Plymouth pilgrims' feast. A year had passed in which over half of the Mayflower passengers had died, including 16 of the 20 adult women. But there was promise of a winter of plenty, and so a feast was held, with the natives and their chief Massasoit contributing the venison. There one would have heard hearty singing of "All people that on earth do dwell," perhaps the most renowned of the early metrical psalms. This hymn versifies Psalm 100: "Old Hundredth" we call both the text and the tune. Musical instruments, forbidden by these strict Calvinists, were unnecessary; these people knew the tune and the words. Later, when times were more lax, a leader would line out the hymn, singing alone each line which was then repeated by the congregation.

William Kethe, a Scottish cleric, published the words to Old Hundredth in 1561. For Kethe, as for Psalm 100, thanksgiving is not an emotional outburst of grateful people or a personal response to economic success. Thanksgiving is the condition of the faithful human creature before God. The celebration of Thanksgiving comes at the end of summer's plenty, but in the face of deathly winter. We praise because "The Lord our God is good." The Puritans sang the biblical word of God, or as close as their doggerel could render it.

And doggerel it was. Recall the third stanza of Old Hundredth: "Approach with joy his courts unto." The *Bay Psalm Book*, the first book printed in Massachusetts, was just as ungainly:

Know that Iehovah he is God,
Who hath us formed it is hee,
& not ourselves: his owne people
& sheepe of his pasture are wee.

Most of our hymnals retain Kethe's wording, not to commend its poetry, but, just as we treasure our grandmother's torn quilt, to honor its memory. But these faltering translations, surrendering poetic beauty to biblical purity, rankled many of the faithful, and none more than Isaac Watts.

The story goes that when a teenager he complained to his father about the infelicity of the lines, and the elder Watts, himself a twice-jailed dissenter, challenged his son with the words, "Give us something better, young man." Watts began writing, and with him began imaginative hymns written in the English language for the Sunday liturgy. A master at versification, he improved the psalter translations, and with the simple excellence of his lines won over the Protestants to sing hymns freed from biblical texts, like his "Alas! and did my Savior bleed" and "When I survey the wondrous cross." My favorite, "Go worship at Emmanuel's feet," is a ballad long forgotten by the churches in which 14 images for Christ are evoked in praise:

> Is he a Tree? The world receives
> salvation from his healing leaves.
> Is he a Door? I'll enter in;
> behold the pastures large and green.
> Is he a Star? he breaks the night,
> piercing the shades with dawning light.

His doxologies give words to our stutter: One of his hymns concludes with praise to the God whom "we adore, that sea of life and love unknown, without a bottom or a shore."

Watts believed that the church should form the Hebrew psalter into Christian praise. He cast Psalm 72 as "Jesus shall reign where'er the sun." Psalm 98 became one of our culture's most popular praises at the arrival of the king of justice and the consequent renewal of the earth: "Joy to the world." Psalm 90, "Lord, you have been our dwelling place in all generations," became the beloved "O God, our help in ages past." In the words of this hymn, we stand small within the mighty creation, our years little within the turning decades and centuries. We will die, as does the fertile summer. Yet we praise our God, our help, our hope. The hymn is objective praise for divine mercy and corporate prayer for God's protection, not thanks for personal or group accomplishment. Its grand tune, the stately Saint Anne, was composed by William Croft in the early eighteenth century and is one melody that can bear majestic musical treatment.

Isaac Watts died on November 25, 1748. Thus we remember his 697 hymns, or at least some of them, around the time of the American Thanksgiving festival. One reason for Christians to assemble on Thanksgiving evening is to sing Psalms 100 and 90: After we join the pilgrims in "All people that on earth do dwell," we'll sing Watts's

"O God, our help in ages past." These hymns give thanks for life in the the face of death. We sing not with the winning football team, but with the four women left alive in Plymouth. Let our weak happiness over acquisitions and accomplishments yield to the vigor of the psalter, the church's original and enduring hymnal.

Let All Mortal Flesh Keep Silence

Let all mortal flesh keep silence,
and with fear and trembling stand;
ponder nothing earthly minded,
for with blessing in his hand
Christ our God to earth descendeth,
our full homage to demand.

King of kings, yet born of Mary,
as of old on earth he stood,
Lord of lords in human vesture,
in the body and the blood,
he will give to all the faithful
his own self for heavenly food.

Rank on rank the host of heaven
spreads its vanguard on the way,
as the Light of Light descendeth
from the realms of endless day,
that the powers of hell may vanish
as the darkness clears away.

At his feet the six-winged seraph,
cherubim with sleepless eye,
veil their faces to the Presence,
as with ceaseless voice they cry,
"Alleluia, alleluia!
Alleluia, Lord Most High!"

Liturgy of St. James, adp. Gerard Moultrie

When I was 20, I told a grand old liturgist about my determination to write modern hymns. Gently he commended to me his favorite hymn, "Let all mortal flesh keep silence." I did not smile then, as I do now, at his subtle wisdom. But that classic hymn, crafted in England during the nineteenth century, from the offertory song in the fourth-century Syrian Liturgy of St. James, taught me some characteristics of a blockbuster hymn. Wed to an accessible tune and enlivened by interesting rhythm, the words, echoing the scriptures and employing archetypal imagery, serve the liturgical assembly by objectively praising God. Our study of classic hymnody began with Anna Hoppe's plea that we, like the man with the speech impediment, will have our tongues loosed for praise. In "let all mortal flesh keep silence," we find words for even our silence.

Whether the hymns we select are over a millenium old or new this year, whether they were written by one of the church's stellar saints or by a hymnal committee, whether we sing the hymn throughout a season or appoint it only once a year: Let the words of our hymns be worth singing. Inspired by the metaphors in the psalter, let our hymnals be treasure chests overflowing with such multi-faceted jewels that it is difficult to choose between the diamond and the opal. An excellent hymn, like a great poem, wants to be memorized. You sing it at the liturgy and are delighted, perhaps even astounded, and you sing it over and over that week until you know its words by heart. You want to join in singing the words, for the words themselves sing.

Here have been 40 intelligent hymns, one for each day as we ride out the flood in our ark; 40 hymns worth singing, doxologies and ballads, chants and carols, chorales and processional hymns, folk songs and marches, all awaiting our strings and pipes. May these hymns, and many others, keep us singing heartily together as long as the rains endure.

CHRONOLOGICAL INDEX

HYMNAL INDEX

	The Hymn Book	Lutheran Book of Worship	The Hymnal 1982	Worship, 3rd ed.	Lead Me, Guide Me	United Methodist Hymnal	Presbyterian Hymnal	Collegeville Hymnal	Songs for a Gospel People
All creatures of our God	1	527	400	520	-	62	455	555	
All glory, laud, and honor	447	108	154	128	30	280	88	256	
All people that on earth	12	245	377	669	304	75	220	-	
All praise to Thee	363	278	43	-	-	682	542	438	
Amazing grace	-	448	671	583	173	378	280	447	
Awake, my soul	357	269	11	-	-	-	456	420	
Camina, pueblo de Dios	-	-	-	-	-	305	296	-	
Christus Paradox	-	-	-	-	-	-	-	-	64
Come down, O Love divine	67	508	516	472	-	475	313	498	
Come, ye faithful	464	132	200	456	-	315	114	279	
For all the saints	501	174	287	705	105	711	526	336	
From heaven above	411	51	80	388	-	-	54	213	
Godhead here is hiding	329	199	314	489	-	-	519	368 369 370	
Good Christian friends	400	55	107	391	-	224	28	190	
Hark, the herald angels sing	407	60	87	387	13	240	31	222	
Hope of the world	-	493	472	565	-	178	360	-	
Jesu, Jesu	-	-	-	431	33	432	367	-	6
Jesus, remember me	-	-	-	423	48	488	599	-	
Jesus, your blood	-	302	-	-	-	-	-	-	
Let all mortal flesh	332	198	324	523	-	626	5	377	

	The Hymn Book	The Lutheran Book of Worship	The Hymnal 1982	Worship, 3rd ed.	Lead Me, Guide Me	United Methodist Hymnal	Presbyterian Hymnal	Collegeville Hymnal	Cantate Domino
Mary the Dawn	-	-	-	-	-	-	-	329	
O come, O come Emmanuel	390	34	56	357	3	211	9	179	
O God, our help	133	320	680	579	230	117	210	457	
O Holy Spirit by whose breath	245 246	164 284 472	501	475 479 482	69 70	651	125	278 297	
O Jesus, joy of loving hearts	343	356	649	605	-	-	510	510	
O Mary, don't you weep	-	-	-	-	134	-	-	-	
O morning star	117	76	496	389	-	247	69	214	
O radiant light	365	279	25 36	12 679	-	686	548 549	436 442	
O splendor of God's glory	-	271	5	-	-	679	474	-	
Simple gifts	-	-	554	-	-	-	-	-	
Sing, my tongue	446	118	166	437	-	296	-	-	
The glory of these forty days	-	-	143	422	32	-	87	-	
The God of Abraham praise	-	544	401	537	-	116	488	-	
There in God's garden	-	-	-	-	-	-	-	-	131
This day God gives me	68	188	370	671 673	-	-	-	305	
Wake, O wake	394	31	61	371	-	720	17	186	
What wondrous love	-	385	439	600	-	292	85	530	
Where true love and charity	-	126	581	598	-	549	-	387	
Ye watchers and ye holy ones	7	175	618	707	104	90	451	578	

SOURCES

The following hymnals were used for the hymn texts in this book:

Cantate Domino
Oxford University Press
London, England

The Collegeville Hymnal
The Liturgical Press
Collegeville, Minnesota

The Hymnal 1982
The Church Hymnal Corporation
New York, New York

Lutheran Book of Worship
Augsburg Publishing House
Minneapolis, Minnesota

The Presbyterian Hymnal
Westminster/John Knox Press
Louisville, Kentucky

Songs for a Gospel People
Wood Lake Books, Inc.
Winfield, BC, V0H 2C0

The United Methodist Hymnal
The United Methodist Publishing House
Nashville, Tennessee

Worship
GIA Publications, Inc.
Chicago, Illinois

All creatures of our God and King. Adaptation copyright © 1989. Reprinted from the *United Methodist Hymnal* [#62] by permission.

All glory, laud, and honor. *The Hymnal*, #154.

All people that on earth do dwell. *United Methodist Hymnal*, #75.

All praise to thee, my God, this night. *United Methodist Hymnal*, #682.

Amazing grace. *United Methodist Hymnal*, #378.

Awake, my soul, and with the sun. *Lutheran Book of Worship*, #269.

Camina, pueblo de Dios. *United Methodist Hymnal*, #305. Nueva Creacion (Camino Pueblo de Dios): copyright © 1979 Cesareo Gabarian. Published by OCP Publications, Portland OR 97213. All rights reserved. Used with permission.

Christus paradox. *Songs for a Gospel People*, #64. Text copyright © Sylvia Dunstan, 1984.

Come down, O love divine. *The Hymnal*, #516.

Come, ye faithful, raise the strain. *United Methodist Hymnal*, #315.

For all the saints. *The Hymnal*, #287.

From heaven above. Text copyright © 1978 Lutheran Book of Worship [#51] Reprinted by permission of Augsburg Fortress.

Godhead here is hiding. *The Collegeville Hymnal*, #368.

Good Christian friends, rejoice. *Lutheran Book of Worship*, #55.

Hark! The herald angels sing. *Worship*, #387.

Hope of the world. *Lutheran Book of Worship*, #493. Text copyright © 1954. Renewal 1982 by The Hymn Society, Texas Christian University, Fort Worth TX 76129. All rights reserved. Used with permission.

Jesu, Jesu. *United Methodist Hymnal*, #432. Copyright © 1969, 1989 by Hope Publishing Company, Carol Stream IL 60188. All rights reserved. Used with permission.

Jesus, your blood and rightousness. *Lutheran Book of Worship*, #302.

Jesus, remember me. *Worship*, #423. Copyright © 1981, Les Presses de Taizé (France). Used by permission of GIA Publications, Inc., Chicago. All rights reserved.

Let all mortal flesh. *The Hymnal*, #324.

Mary the dawn. *The Collegeville Hymnal*, #329. Copyright © 1949 McLaughlin and Reilly, a division of Summy-Birchard, Inc. This piece is from *Seasonal Hymns of the Liturgy.* All Rights Reserved. Used with permission.

O come, O come, Emmanuel. *The Hymnal*, #56.

O God, our help in ages past. *The Hymnal*, #680.

O Holy Spirit, by whose breath. *The Hymnal*, #501. Text copyright © 1971, John Webster Grant.

O Jesus, joy of loving hearts. *The Collegeville Hymnal*, #510.

O Mary, don't you weep. *United Methodist Hymnal*, #134.

O morning star, how fair and bright! Text copyright © 1978 Lutheran Book of Worship [#76]. Reprinted by permission of Augsburg Fortress.

O radiant light. *Worship*, #12. Text copyright © William Storey; Acc. © 1975 GIA Publications, Inc.

O splendor of God's glory bright. *The Presbyterian Hymnal*, #474.

The glory of these forty days. *Worship*, #422.

The God of Abraham praise. *Lutheran Book of Worship*, #544.

There in God's garden. *Cantate Domino*, #131. Copyright © 1976 by Hinshaw Music, Inc. Used with permission.

This day God gives me. *Worship*, #673. Text copyright © 1969, James Quinn, SJ. Reprinted by permission of Geoffrey Chapman, a division of Cassell PLC.

'Tis the gift to be simple. *The Hymnal*, #554.

Wake, O wake, and sleep no longer. *Worship*, #371. Text copyright © 1982 Hope Publishing Co., Carol Stream IL 60188. All rights reserved. Used with permission.

What wondrous love is this. *United Methodist Hymnal*, #292.

Where true love and charity are found. *Worship*, #598. Text copyright © 1975 GIA Publications, Inc., Chicago. All rights reserved. Used with permission.

Ye watchers and ye holy ones. *The Hymnal*, #618. Reprinted by permission of Oxford University Press.

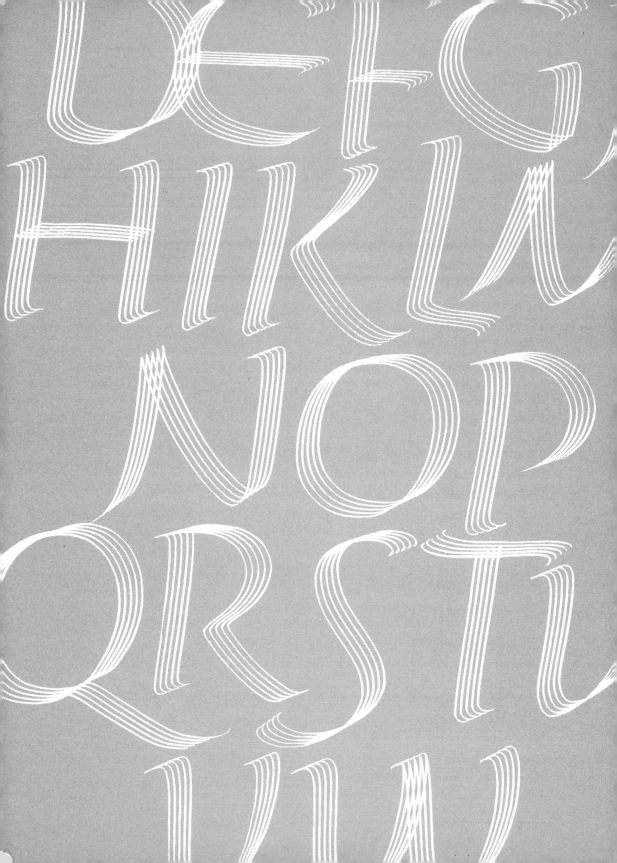